BIG BOOK OF
INSULTS

BIG BOOK OF
INSULTS

Nancy Mcphee

CHANCELLOR
PRESS

First published in Great Britain 1982 by Book Club Associates by
arrangement with Andre Deutsch Limited under the title
The Complete Book of Insults

This is a combined volume of *The Book of Insults Ancient and Modern*,
revised edition, published by the Paddington Press Limited in 1979 and
The Second Book of Insults first published by Andre Deutsch Limited in
1981. Previously published as *The Bumper book of Insults!* by Chancellor
Press.

This 2001 edition published by Chancellor Press an imprint of
Bounty Books, a division of Octopus Publishing Group,
2-4 Heron Quays, London, E14 4JP
Reprinted 2002
Copyright © 1978, 1979, 1981 by Nancy McPhee

ISBN 0 7537 0456 0

Printed and bound in Finland

Contents

To my family,
without whose solicitous concern
and helpful suggestions
this book would have been finished
in half the time.

ACKNOWLEDGEMENTS

The author wishes to thank the following for permission to reprint material included in this book: A&W Publishers, Inc. for extracts from *The Book of Days* by Elizabeth Donaldson and Gerald Donaldson. Abelard-Schuman Ltd. for extracts from *I Wish I'd Said That* by Kenneth Edwards, and for extracts from *I Wish I'd Said That Too!* by Kenneth Edwards. George Allen & Unwin Publishers Ltd. for extracts from *Quote... Unquote* by Nigel Rees. Brandt & Brandt Literary Agents, Inc. for extracts from *The Age of Wellington* copyright © 1963 by Leonard Cooper. Cassell Ltd. for extracts from *The Five Hundred Best English Letters*, edited by Frederick Edwin Smith Birkenhead. Citadel Press for extracts from *The Algonquin Wits* by Robert Drennon, published by arrangement with Lyle Stuart Inc. William Collins Sons & Co. Canada Ltd. for an extract from *Colombo's Hollywood* by John Robert Colombo. Delacorte Press for extracts from *Dictionary of Quotations* by Bergen Evans, and for extracts from *The Hater's Handbook* by Joseph Rosner. The *Detroit Free Press* for a comment by Ronald Reagan. Dodd, Mead & Co. for extracts from *The Home Book of Quotations* edited by Burton Stevenson, and for extracts from *The Home Book of Humorous Quotations,* edited by A.K. Adams. E.P. Dutton Publishing Co. Inc. for extracts from *The Fine Art of Political Wit* by Leonard A. Harris. Eyre & Spottiswoode Publishers Ltd. for extracts from *More Invective* by Hugh Kingsmill, and for extracts from *An Anthology of Invective and Abuse* by Hugh Kingsmill. John Stevenson Publisher for extracts from *Insults — A Practical Anthology* by Max Herzberg, published originally by Greystone Press. Harper & Row, Publishers, Inc. for extracts from *A Treasury of Humorous Quotations* by Herbert V. Prochnow, for extracts from *Collections & Recollections I* by G.W.E. Russell, originally published by Harper & Brothers, and for extracts from *The Smith of Smiths* by Hesketh Pearson, originally published by Harper & Brothers. William Heinemann Ltd. A.P. Watt for extracts from *Lives of The Wits* by Hesketh Pearson, for extracts from *The Soul of Wit* by George Rostrevor Hamilton. Hurtig Publishers Ltd. for extracts from *Colombo's Little Book of Canadian Proverbs, Graffiti, Limericks and Other Vital Matters* by John Robert Colombo. Alfred A. Knopf, Inc. for extracts from *A New Dictionary of Quotations* by H.L. Mencken, and for extracts from *The Dictionary of Biographical Quotations* by Richard Kenin & Justin Wintle. Macmillan Publishing Co. Inc. for extracts from *The Last Word* by Louis Kronenberger, and for extracts from *The Second Post* edited by Edward Verall Lucas. Methuen & Co. Ltd. for an extract from *The Gentlest Art,* edited by Edward Verall Lucas, and for extracts from *A Book of Famous Wits* by Walter Copeland Jerrold. Oxford University Press for extracts from *Selected Letters of Sydney Smith*, edited by Nowell C. Smith. Penguin Books Ltd. for extracts from *Penguin Dictionary of Quotations* by J.M. Cohen and M.J. Cohen, published by Allen Lane. G.P. Putnam's Sons for extracts from *The Wit and Wisdom of Sydney Smith* by Sydney Smith. The Warden and Fellows of Nuffield College, Oxford for extracts from *William Cobbett* by James Sambrook. Rutgers University Press for extracts from *William Cobbett: His Thoughts & His Times* copyright © 1966 by John W. Osborne. Charles Scribner's Sons for an extract from *Nineteenth Century English Letters*, edited by Byron Johnson Rees.

Although every effort has been made to ensure that permissions for all material were obtained, those sources not formally acknowledged here will be included in all future editions of this book.

Foreword

From time immemorial, men have relished the delights of verbal warfare. It is a paradox of our own inarticulate age that this enjoyment of a clever insult has never been higher. Having largely lost our interest in using language with precision and imagination, we hide our real thoughts behind fuzzy words and a mealy mouth — but we secretly admire those who have the courage to say aloud what we ourselves only dare to think!

No doubt there are profound and Freudian reasons for this malicious pleasure; but whatever the explanation, the immense popularity of television and nightclub comedians who specialize in the blunt put-down demonstrates that verbal violence strikes a deep and responsive chord. The sad fact that so many of these performers are graceless and vulgar does not seem to lessen their appeal, although it does highlight a deplorable decline in the art of invective.

For there was a golden age, not so long ago, when insult was indeed an art; when people had strong opinions and were only too ready to voice them. Over the years there have been many who called a spade a spade with imagination, wit and style.

This modest collection of boos and catcalls has tried to bring together some of the best of these. Connoisseurs of the art will recognize many famous broadsides, and note the absence of others. My choices were highly personal and no doubt eccentric. What they have in common is a deft and uninhibited use of language, all too often missing today.

Still, those of us who cherish this black side of literature should not be too pessimistic. There are enough contemporary examples of inventive insult to encourage the hope that the tide may yet be turned. If this collection can both amuse and inspire its readers to a more creative use of invective, it will have served its purpose.

N.G.M.
1978

HIS MIND WAS LIKE A SOUP DISH— WIDE AND SHALLOW...

IRVING STONE ON
WM. JENNINGS BRYAN

I'LL TICKLE YOUR CATASTROPHE

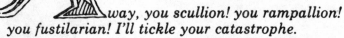*way, you scullion! you rampallion!*
you fustilarian! I'll tickle your catastrophe.

William Shakespeare (1564-1616)
King Henry IV, Second Part

Throughout the centuries, human beings have exercized their highest powers of invention and wit in speaking ill of one another. That leaven of malice which exists in all of us has been exalted in some people almost to the point of genius; and thousands of otherwise amiable souls have risen to the occasional pointed put-down or audacious phrase which the world has relished enough to note and long remember.

One can turn to the Bible for inspiration in many things — among them, the use of a rather mild form of invective:

> *O generation of vipers, who hath warned you to flee from the wrath to come?*
>
> Matthew 3:7

> *Ye blind guides, which strain at a gnat, and swallow a camel.*
>
> Matthew 23:24

> *Because thou art lukewarm and neither cold nor hot, I will spue thee out of my mouth.*
>
> Revelations 3:16

> *A whip for the horse, a bridle for the ass, and a rod for the fool's back.*
>
> Proverbs 26:3

The ancient Romans were never afraid to be uncomplimentary; the poet Martial made a career of it:

> *I could do without your face, Chloë, and without your neck, and your hands, and your limbs, and, to*

16

save myself the trouble of mentioning the points in detail, I could do without you altogether.

Marcus Valerius Martial (c.40-104 AD)

Nycilla dyes her locks, 'tis said,
But 'tis a foul aspersion;
She buys them black; they therefore need
No subsequent immersion.

Marcus Valerius Martial (c.40-104 AD)

Strong language has always sat well in the mouths of **strong** and powerful men. One such person with firm opinions and a caustic tongue was King James I of England. James, who considered himself an expert in a variety of fields, earnestly attempted to suppress a habit which has yet to be wiped out by a succession of similar exhortations:

> *... And for the vanities committed in this filthie custome, is it not both great vanitie and uncleannesse, that at the table, a place of respect, of cleanlinesse, of modestie, men should not be ashamed, to sit tossing of Tobacco pipes, and puffing of the smoke of Tobacco one to another, making the filthy smoke and stinke thereof, to exhale athwart the dishes, and infect the aire, when very often men that abhorre it are at their repast? ... it makes a kitchin also often-times in the inward parts of men, soiling and infecting them, with an unctuous and oily kinde of Soote, as hath bene found in some great Tobacco takers, that after their death were opened.*

> *... Have you not reason then to bee ashamed, and to forbeare this filthie noveltie ... a custome loathsome to the eye, hatefull to the nose, harmefull to the braine, dangerous to the Lungs, and in the blacke stinking fume thereof, neerest resembling the horrible Stigian smoke of the pit that is bottomlesse.*

King James I of England (1566-1625)
A Counterblaste to Tobacco

17

Invective and abuse turns up in even less likely places than the essays of a scholar-king. The man who imported tobacco into Europe, Sir Walter Raleigh, met a sticky end: for this and other sins he was hanged, drawn and quartered. Such harsh punishment may have come almost as a relief after his subjection, during his trial, to this incredible tirade:

> *I will prove you the notoriousest traitor that ever come to the bar. ... thou art a monster; thou hast an English face, but a Spanish heart. ... Thou art the most vile and execrable Traitor that ever lived. ... I want words sufficient to express thy viperous Treasons. ... Thou art an odious fellow, thy name is hateful to all the realm of England. ... There never lived a viler viper upon the face of the earth than thou.*
>
> Sir Edward Coke (1552-1634)
> To Sir Walter Raleigh

Such verbal pyrotechnics were by no means rare. One of the joys of true invective, for both practitioner and audience, is the opportunity for the imagination to soar in flights of bombast. Some creative critics have been punch-drunk with words:

> *Cut-purses, miles of cheats, enterprises of scoundrels, delicious disgusts, foolish decisions, crippled hopes, virile women, effeminate men, and everywhere the love of gold.*
>
> Giordano Bruno (c.1548-1600)
> On his life and times

> *You common cry of curs! whose breath I hate*
> *As reek o' the rotten fens, whose loves I prize*
> *As the dead carcases of unburied men*
> *That do corrupt the air.*
>
> William Shakespeare (1564-1616)
> *Coriolanus*

> *Vain Nashe, railing Nashe, cracking Nashe, bibbing Nashe, baggage Nashe, swaddish Nashe, roguish Nashe ... the swish-swash of the press, the bum of impudency, the shambles of beastliness*

. . . the toadstool of the realm. . . .
Gabriel Harvey (1545-1630)
On Thomas Nashe

The gentle Charles Lamb suffered the sad fate of many a playwright when his new play was hissed on its first night. So violent was the audience's reaction that Lamb joined in the hissing himself, lest he be mistaken for the author! Describing the scene to a friend, Lamb later unleashed an uncharacteristic torrent of venom:

> *Mercy on us, that God should give his favourite children, men, mouths to speak with, discourse rationally, to promise smoothly, to flatter agreeably, to encourage warmly, to counsel wisely: to sing with, to drink with, and to kiss with: and that they should turn them into mouths of adders, bears, wolves, hyenas, and whistle like tempests, and emit breath through them like distillations of aspic poison, to asperse and vilify the innocent labour of their fellow creatures who are desirous to please them. God be pleased to make the breath stink and the teeth rot out of them all therefore!*

Charles Lamb (1775-1834)

One of the greatest comic characters in all literature, Sir John Falstaff, had his many deficiencies catalogued by his creator:

> *Why dost thou converse with that trunk of humours, that bolting-hutch of beastliness, that swoln parcel of dropsies, that huge bombard of sack, that stuffed cloakbag of guts, that roasted Manningtree ox with the pudding in his belly, that reverend vice, that grey iniquity, that father ruffian, that vanity in years?*

William Shakespeare (1564-1616)
King Henry IV, Second Part

Some fastidious cursers discover that words in common use cannot express their incoherent anger—they take refuge in the obscure, or even make up their own!

19

A blatant Bassarid of Boston, a rampant Maenad of Massachusetts.

Algernon Swinburne (1837-1909)
On Harriet Beecher Stowe

This dodipoule, this didopper... Why, thou arrant butter whore, thou cotqueane & scrattop of scoldes, wilt thou never leave afflicting a dead Carcasse... a wispe, a wispe, rippe, rippe, you kitchin-stuff wrangler!

Thomas Nashe (1567-1601)
On Gabriel Harvey

A gap-toothed and hoary-headed ape ... who now in his dotage spits and chatters from a dirtier perch of his own finding and fouling: coryphaeus or choragus of his Bulgarian tribe of autocoprophagous baboons ...

Algernon Swinburne (1837-1909)
On Ralph Waldo Emerson

A freakish homunculus germinated outside lawful procreation.

Henry Arthur Jones (1851-1929)
On Bernard Shaw

A Byzantine logothete.

Theodore Roosevelt (1858-1919)
On Woodrow Wilson

Calling them slubberdegullion druggles ... ninny lobcocks, scurvy sneaksbies ... noddy meacocks, blockish grutnols, doddi-pol jolt-heads, jobbernol goosecaps ... flutch calf-lollies, grouthead gnatsnappers, lob-dotterels... codshead loobies, ninnie-hammer fly-catchers ... and other such like defamatory epithets.

François Rabelais (c. 1490-1553)

A warts-and-all description of a person's physical characteristics has always been an effective way of being unpleasant:

With leering Looks, Bull-fac'd, and freckl'd fair,
With two left legs, and Judas-color'd Hair,

And frowzy Pores that taint the ambient Air.

John Dryden (1631-1700)
On Jacob Tonson, a publisher

They brought one Pinch, a hungry lean-fac'd villain,
A mere anatomy, a mountebank,
A threadbare juggler, and a fortune-teller,
A needy, hollow-ey'd, sharp-looking wretch,
A living dead man.

William Shakespeare (1564-1616)
The Comedy of Errors

Why don't you get a haircut? You look like a chrysanthemum.

P.G. Wodehouse (1881-1975)

He's a little man, that's his trouble. Never trust a man with short legs—brains too near their bottoms.

Noel Coward (1899-1973)

Other naysayers can describe their victims almost tangibly with the word-pictures they draw:

The English country-gentleman galloping after a fox—the unspeakable in full pursuit of the uneatable.

Oscar Wilde (1854-1900)

His mind is a muskeg of mediocrity.

John Macnaughton (1858-1943)
On an anonymous Canadian professor

A louse in the locks of literature.

Alfred, Lord Tennyson (1809-1894)
On critic Churton Collins

His mind was like a soup dish, wide and shallow; it could hold a small amount of nearly anything, but the slightest jarring spilled the soup into somebody's lap.

Irving Stone (b. 1903)
On William Jennings Bryan

O hideous little bat, the size of snot.
> Karl Shapiro (b. 1913)
> *The Fly*

His mind was a kind of extinct sulphur-pit.
> Thomas Carlyle (1795-1881)
> On Napoleon III

He was the mildest manner'd man
That ever scuttled ship or cut a throat.
> Lord Byron (1788-1824)

He is like trying to pick up mercury with a fork.
> Lloyd George (1863-1945)
> On Eamon de Valera

My handwriting looks as if a swarm of ants, escaping from an ink bottle, had walked over a sheet of paper without wiping their legs.
> Sydney Smith (1771-1845)

Subtler souls find the gentle touch effective:

Why do you sit there looking like an envelope without any address on it?
> Mark Twain (1835-1910)

I like him and his wife. He is so ladylike, and she is such a perfect gentleman.
> Sydney Smith (1771-1845)

To mankind in general, Macbeth and Lady Macbeth stand out as the supreme type of all that a host and hostess should not be.
> Max Beerbohm (1872-1956)

Funny without being vulgar.
> Sir Herbert Beerbohm
> Tree (1853-1917)
> On his own performance as Hamlet

You and I were long friends; you are now my enemy, and I am

> *Yours,*
> *B. Franklin*

> Benjamin Franklin (1706-1790)
> Letter to William Strahan

Still others enjoy a play on words:

He has impeccable bad taste.

Otis Ferguson

Very nice, though there are dull stretches.

Antoine de Rivarol (1753-1801)
On a two-line poem

If only he'd wash his neck, I'd wring it.

John Sparrow

The man who could call a spade a spade should be compelled to use one. It is the only thing he is fit for.

Oscar Wilde (1854-1900)

The tightly-knit literary and artistic communities of the past often led to strong personal animosities and yielded a rich vein of personal abuse:

Of course we all know that Morris was a wonderful all-round man, but the act of walking round him has always tired me.

Max Beerbohm (1872-1956)
On William Morris

Rossini would have been a great composer if his teacher had spanked him enough on his backside.

Ludwig van Beethoven (1770-1827)

Poor Matt. He's gone to heaven, no doubt—but he won't like God.

Robert Louis Stevenson (1850-1894)
On Matthew Arnold

Henry James was one of the nicest old ladies I ever met.

William Faulkner (1897-1962)

Thackeray settled like a meat-fly on whatever one had got for dinner, and made one sick of it.

John Ruskin (1819-1900)

Every once in a while someone achieved the perfect squelch:

Your manuscript is both good and original; but the

*part that is good is not original, and the part that is
original is not good.*

Samuel Johnson (1709-1784)

*You may have genius. The contrary is, of course,
probable.*

Oliver Wendell Holmes (1841-1935)

*From the moment I picked your book up until I laid
it down I was convulsed with laughter. Some day I
intend reading it.*

Groucho Marx (b. 1895)

Periodically, a new art form is invented and turned to
unkind uses. E.C. Bentley, the detective-story writer,
devised the clerihew:

*Geoffrey Chaucer
Took a bath (in a saucer)
In consequence of certain hints
Dropped by the Black Prince.*

E. Clerihew Bentley (1875-1956)

The use of the formal curse reaches back into unrecorded
history, and is still in vogue in parts of the world today.
The mediaeval church laid this heavy imprecation on the
heads of its excommunicated sinners:

*Let him be damned in his going out and coming in.
The Lord strike him with madness and blindness.
May the heavens empty upon him thunderbolts and
the wrath of the Omnipotent burn itself unto him in
the present and future world. May the Universe
light against him and the earth open to swallow
him up.*

Pope Clement VI (1478-1534)

The traditional Gypsy curse chilled Europeans for years:

*May you wander over the face of the earth forever,
never sleep twice in the same bed, never drink water
twice from the same well, and never cross the same
river twice in a year.*

24

while curses from esoteric corners of the earth could be bloodcurdling:

> *Die, may he: Tiger, catch him; Snake, bite him; Steep hill, fall down on him; River, flow over him; Wild boar, bite him.*
>
> Ceremonial curse of the Todas of India

> *May you dig up your father by moonlight and make soup of his bones.*
>
> Fiji Islands

or merely uncomfortable:

> *May the fleas of a thousand camels infest your armpits.*
>
> Arab curse

> *May your left ear wither and fall into your right pocket.*
>
> Arab curse

> *May you melt off the earth like snow off the ditch.*
>
> Irish curse

> *May the curse of Mary Malone and her nine blind illegitimate children chase you so far over the hills of Damnation that the Lord himself can't find you with a telescope.*
>
> Irish curse

The Chinese and the Scots were struck with the same philosophical thought:

> *May you be born in an important time.*
>
> Confucius (c.551-478 BC)

> *May you live in interesting times.*
>
> Old Scottish curse

and a host of more recent imitators have shown more or less ingenuity:

> *May she marry a ghost, and bear him a kitten, and may the High King of Glory permit it to get the mange.*
>
> James Stephens (1882-1950)

25

I would thou didst itch from head to foot and I had the scratching of thee.

William Shakespeare (1564-1616)
Troilus and Cressida

May you be cursed with a chronic anxiety about the weather.

John Burroughs (1837-1921)

The real test of the creative insult is its use in conversation. Which of us has not thought of the perfect response — twenty-four hours too late? The witty retort has always been enjoyed and frequently recorded:

THE EARL OF SANDWICH: *Egad, sir, I do not know whether you will die on the gallows or of the pox.*
JOHN WILKES: *That will depend, my Lord, on whether I embrace your principles or your mistress.*

John Wilkes (1727-1797)

*
CLERGYMAN: *How did you like my sermon, Mr. Canning?*
CANNING: *You were brief.*
CLERGYMAN: *Yes, you know I avoid being tedious.*
CANNING: *But you* were *tedious.*

George Canning (1770-1827)

The quick-witted responses of Winston Churchill have become legendary:

LADY ASTOR: *Winston, if you were my husband, I should flavour your coffee with poison.*
CHURCHILL: *Madam, if I were your husband, I should drink it.*
*
BESSIE BRADDOCK, M.P.: *Winston, you're drunk!*
CHURCHILL: *Bessie, you're ugly. And tomorrow morning I shall be sober.*

Bernard Shaw once sent Churchill two tickets for the opening of his new play, with the invitation:

Bring a friend — if you have one.

Churchill regretted that he was engaged, and asked for tickets for the second performance:

G.B. SHAW

If there is one.

Winston Churchill (1874-1965)

Dorothy Parker was seldom caught with her wits down:

> CLARE BOOTHE LUCE *(meeting Parker in a doorway):*
> *Age before beauty!*
> DOROTHY PARKER *(gliding through the door):* **Pearls**
> **before swine!**

Dorothy Parker (1893-1967)

To speak ill of the dead is, of course, the ultimate form of insult; and no doubt this is one reason for the popularity of the epitaph. One such relic from mediaeval Italy celebrates a man who was a notorious and vicious gossip:

> *Here lies Aretino, Tuscan poet*
> *Who spoke evil of everyone but God,*
> *Giving the excuse, "I never knew Him."*

Anonymous

Some writers of epitaphs are cutting and cruel; here is Lord Byron on a contemporary politician:

With death doomed to grapple
Beneath this cold slab, he
Who lied in the Chapel
Now lies in the Abbey.

Lord Byron (1788-1824)
On William Pitt

Some are sarcastic, as in this epitaph on an inattentive waiter:

By and by
God caught his eye.

David McCord (b. 1897)

and some are frivolous:

Excuse my dust.

This one's on me.

Dorothy Parker (1893-1967)
Suggested epitaphs

But none of these is as heartfelt as the genuine epitaph on a tombstone in the churchyard at Horsley-Down, Cumberland, erected in less than loving memory to "Mary, wife of Thomas Bond" by her brother-in-law:

She was proud, peevish and passionate ...
Her behaviour was discreet toward strangers
But
Independent in her family ...
She was a professed enemy to flattery,
and was seldom known to praise or commend ...
The talents in which she principally excelled
Were difference of opinion, and discovering
flaws and imperfections ...
She sometimes made her husband happy ...
But
Much more frequently miserable ...
Insomuch that in 30 years cohabitation he ...
had not in the whole, enjoyed two years
of matrimonial comfort.
At length

*Finding that she had lost the affections of her
    husband,
        As well as the regard of her neighbours,
Family disputes having been divulged by servants,
    She died of vexation, July 20, 1768
        Aged 48 years.*

The late Mistress Bond was only one of many women who
have been maligned through the ages:

She never was really charming till she died.

Terence (c.185-159 BC)

*God created Adam lord of all living creatures, but
Eve spoiled it all.*

Martin Luther (1483-1546)

Many men have shared Luther's opinion about women:

*Nature intended women to be our slaves. . . . they
are our property; we are not theirs. They belong to
us, just as a tree that bears fruit belongs to a
gardener. What a mad idea to demand equality for
women ! . . . Women are nothing but machines for
producing children.*

Napoleon Bonaparte (1769-1821)

*A woman is only a woman,
But a good cigar is a smoke.*

Rudyard Kipling (1865-1936)

and have expended a good deal of energy in detailing
their deficiencies:

*Nature, I say, doth paynt them further to be weak,
fraile, impacient, feble, and foolishe; and experience
hath declared them to be unconstant, variable,
cruell, and lacking the spirit of counsel and regiment.*

John Knox (1505-1575)
The First Blast of the Trumpet Against
the Monstrous Regiment of Women

The five worst infirmities that afflict the female are

indocility, discontent, slander, jealousy and silli-
ness.
Confucian Marriage Manual

The English Puritans considered their young women to be gad-abouts:

> *The dissolutenesse of our lascivious, impudent, rattle-pated gadding females now is such ... they are lowde and stubborne; their feet abide not in their houses; now they are without, now in the streets, and lie in wait at every corner; being never well pleased nor contented, but when they are wandering abroad to Playes, to Playhouses, Dancing-Matches, Masques, and publicke Shewes.*
William Prynne (1600-1669)

The straight-laced Mr. Prynne was horrified at the modern fashion of shingling women's hair:

> *Even nature herselfe abhors to see a woman shorne or polled; a woman with cut hair is a filthy spectacle, and much like a monster; and all repute it a very great absurdity for a woman to walke abrode with shorne hair; for this is all one as if she should take upon her the forme or person of a man, to whom short cut haire is proper, it being naturall and comly to women to nourish their haire, which even God and nature have given them for a covering, a token of their subjection, and a natural badge to distinguish them from men.*
William Prynne (1600-1669)

And although most men have agreed that marriage is women's proper role in life, they have seldom had a good word to say for it:

> *I have always thought that every woman should marry, and no man.*
Benjamin Disraeli (1804-1881)

> *Strange to say what delight we married people have to see these poor fools decoyed into our condition.*
Samuel Pepys (1633-1703)

Alas! Another instance of the triumph of hope over experience.

Samuel Johnson (1709-1784)
On the remarriage of a widower

Marriage makes an end of many short follies— being one long stupidity.

Friedrich Nietzsche (1844-1900)

Nevertheless, a woman who aspired to anything other than marriage was considered something of an oddity:

A man is in general better pleased when he has a good dinner upon his table than when his wife talks Greek.

Samuel Johnson (1709-1784)

Sir, a woman's preaching is like a dog's walking on his hind legs. It is not done well; but you are surprised to find it done at all.

Samuel Johnson (1709-1784)

I consider that women who are authors, lawyers and politicians are monsters.

Pierre Auguste Renoir (1840-1919)

There are no women composers, never have been and possibly never will be.

Sir Thomas Beecham (1879-1961)

In spite of all this condescension, however, Women's Lib may be said to have arrived:

Twenty million young women rose to their feet with the cry "We will not be dictated to," and promptly became stenographers.

G.K. Chesterton (1874-1936)

and women are determined to have the last word.

Whatever women do they must do twice as well as men to be thought half as good. Luckily, this is not difficult.

Charlotte Whitton (1896-1975)
Former mayor of Ottawa

There is no subject under the sun which has not at some time been the target of derogatory comment.

Not surprisingly, a great deal has been said on the subject of friendship and enmity:

My friends! There are no friends.

Aristotle (384-322 BC)

I have no trouble with my enemies. But my goddam friends, White, they are the ones that keep me walking the floor nights.

Warren G. Harding (1865-1923)
To William A. White

It takes your enemy and your friend, working together, to hurt you to the heart; the one to slander you, and the other to get the news to you.

Mark Twain (1835-1910)

My prayer to God is a very short one: "O Lord, make my enemies ridiculous." God has granted it.

Voltaire (1694-1778)

One should forgive one's enemies, but not before they are hanged.

Heinrich Heine (1797-1856)

I do desire we may be better strangers.

William Shakespeare (1564-1616)
As You Like It

I do not love thee, Doctor Fell,
The reason why I cannot tell;
But this I know, and know full well,
I do not love thee, Doctor Fell.

Thomas Brown (1663-1704)
Translation of an epigram of Martial

The telling of untruths has always occasioned a certain amount of displeasure:

Lord, Lord, how this world is given to lying!

William Shakespeare (1564-1616)
King Henry IV, First Part

I said in my haste, All men are liars.

Psalm 116:11

I denounce Mr. Bernard De Voto as a fool and a tedious and egotistical fool, as a liar and a pompous and boresome liar.

Sinclair Lewis (1885-1951)

They have committed false report; moreover, they have spoken untruths; secondarily, they are slanders; sixth and lastly, they have belied a lady; thirdly, they have verified unjust things; and to conclude, they are lying knaves.

William Shakespeare (1564-1616)
Much Ado About Nothing

To the first charge Your Excellency I answer that it is a lie, to the second charge I say that it is a damned lie, and to the third charge that it is a damned infernal lie, and Your Excellency I have no more to say.

Thomas Tremlett
Chief Justice of Newfoundland, replying
to charges of corruption 1811

The world has castigated its wise men:

The more I read him, the less I wonder that they poisoned him.

Thomas Babington Macaulay (1800-1859)
On Socrates

Take from him his sophisms, futilities and incomprehensibilities and what remains? His foggy mind.

Thomas Jefferson (1743-1826)
On Plato

Plato is a bore.

Friedrich Nietzsche (1844-1900)

and, of course, its fools:

Now, the Lord lighten thee! Thou art a great fool.

William Shakespeare (1564-1616)
King Henry IV, Second Part

We, my Lords, may thank Heaven that we have
something better than our brains to depend on.

Lord Chesterfield (1694-1773)
To the House of Lords

They never open their mouths without subtracting
from the sum of human knowledge.

Thomas Reed (1839-1902)
Speaker of the U.S. House of Representatives
On members of Congress

They say there's but five upon this isle; we are three
of them; if th' other two be brain'd like us, the state
totters.

William Shakespeare (1564-1616)
The Tempest

Even the alphabet has come under attack!

Thou whoreson zed! thou unnecessary letter!

William Shakespeare (1564-1616)
King Lear

Man's stomach has always been near his heart, and food
and drink have occasioned a great deal of verbal as well
as physical indigestion. Geoffrey Chaucer was among the
first to warn of the dangers of overeating:

O wombe! O bely! O stynkyng cod,
Fulfilled of dong and of corrupcioun!
At either ende of thee foul is the soun.

Geoffrey Chaucer (1340-1400)

They have digged their grave with their teeth.

Thomas Adams (1612-1653)

Certain vegetables have been considered less than
desirable:

Parsley
Is gharsley.

Ogden Nash (1902-1971)

Cauliflower is nothing but cabbage with a college
education.

Mark Twain (1835-1910)

A cucumber should be well sliced, and dressed with pepper and vinegar, and then thrown out, as good for nothing.

Samuel Johnson (1704-1789)

MOTHER: *It's broccoli, dear.*
CHILD: *I say it's spinach, and I say the hell with it.*

E.B. White (b. 1899)
Caption to cartoon by Carl Rose

Boiled cabbage à l'Anglaise is something compared with which steamed coarse newsprint bought from bankrupt Finnish salvage dealers and heated over smoky oil stoves is an exquisite delicacy. Boiled British cabbage is something lower than ex-Army blankets stolen by dispossessed Goanese dosshousekeepers who used them to cover busted-down hen houses in the slum district of Karachi, found them useless, threw them in anger into the Indus, where they were recovered by convicted beachcombers with grappling irons, who cut them in strips with shears and stewed them in sheep dip before they were sold to dying beggars. Boiled cabbage!

William Connor (Cassandra) (1909-1967)

Unsatisfactory dinner parties have been the cause of much grief:

This was a good dinner enough, to be sure; but it was not a dinner to ask a man to.

Samuel Johnson (1704-1789)

They make a rare Soop they call Pepper-Pot; its an excellent Breakfast for a Salamander, or a good preparative for a Mountebanks Agent, who Eats Fire one day, that he may get better Victuals the next. Three Spoonfuls so Inflam'd my Mouth, that had I devour'd a Peck of Horse-Radish, and Drank after it a Gallon of Brandy and Gunpowder, I could not have been more importunate for a Drop of Water to cool my Tongue.

Edward Ward (1667-1731)

A particularly bad review was forthcoming if the dinner speaker was poor:

I don't know whether Phoebus fled from the dinner table of Thyestes: at any rate, Ligurinus, we fell from yours. Splendid, indeed, it is, and magnificently supplied with good things; but when you recite you spoil it all. I don't want you to set before me a turbot or a two-pound mullet; I don't want your mushrooms or your oysters. I want you to keep your mouth shut!

Marcus Valerius Martial (c. 40-104 AD)

A preoccupation with appropriate behavior at the dinner table has always been a mark of polite society:

Being set at the table, scratch not thyself, and take thou heed as much as thou can'st to spit, cough and to blow at thy nose; but if it be needful, do it dexterously without much noise, turning thy face sideling.

Frances Hawkins
Youth's Behaviour, 1663

An eminent preacher could not understand the fuss about special foods—

Why is not a rat as good as a rabbit? Why should men eat shrimps and neglect cockroaches?

Henry Ward Beecher (1813-1887)

a solution which may have been forced on the composer of this sad little table-grace:

*Heavenly Father, bless us
And keep us all alive,
There's ten of us to dinner,
And not enough for five.*

Anonymous
Hodge's Grace c.1850

It goes without saying that the imbibing of too much strong drink has always been roundly condemned:

Woe to you that are mighty to drink wine, and stout men at drunkenness.

Isaiah 5:22

Whiskey and vermouth cannot meet as friends, and the Manhattan is an offense against piety.

Bernard De Voto (1897-1956)

A variety of other concoctions has been substituted for whiskey and wine; but none of them, it seems, is without its detractors:

Cocoa is a cad and coward,
Cocoa is a vulgar beast.

G.K. Chesterton (1874-1936)

Free yourselves from the slavery of tea and coffee and other slopkettle.

William Cobbett (1762-1835)

Why do they always put mud into coffee on board steamers? Why does the tea generally taste of boiled boots?

William Makepeace Thackeray (1811-1863)

Heaven sent us Soda Water
As a torment for our crimes.

G.K. Chesterton (1874-1936)

The world of the arts provides a fertile vineyard for sour grapes. Those who follow the craft of writing seldom have a good word to say for it:

No one but a blockhead ever wrote, except for money.

Samuel Johnson (1704-1789)

Novels are receipts to make a whore.

Matthew Greene (1696-1737)

but everyone agrees that writers, and indeed all artists, are ruthless in pursuing their work:

If a writer has to rob his mother, he will not hesitate; the "Ode on a Grecian Urn" is worth any number of old ladies.

William Faulkner (1897-1962)

The true artist will let his wife starve, his children go barefoot, his mother drudge for his living at seventy, sooner than work at anything but his art.

Bernard Shaw (1856-1950)

Too often this diligence is not rewarded by the appreciation of others. Musicians, particularly, bear the brunt of constant criticism. The importance of music has often been downgraded:

He knew music was Good, but it didn't sound right.

George Ade (1866-1944)

Hell is full of musical amateurs.
Music is the brandy of the damned.

Bernard Shaw (1856-1950)

Perhaps it was because Nero played the fiddle, they burned Rome.

Oliver Herford (1863-1935)

and some musical instruments frowned upon:

He was a fiddler, and consequently a rogue.

Jonathan Swift (1667-1745)

The vile squeaking of his wry-necked fife.

William Shakespeare (1564-1616)

including the favorite of the Scots:

... Others, when the bag-pipe sings i' the nose, Cannot contain their urine.

William Shakespeare (1564-1616)
The Merchant of Venice

Often musicians themselves have not been held in high esteem. One who endured the jeers and hoots of his contemporaries was the composer Richard Wagner:

I like Wagner's music better than any other music. It is so loud that one can talk the whole time without people hearing what one says. That is a great advantage.

Oscar Wilde (1854-1900)

Wagner, thank the fates, is no hypocrite. He says right out what he means, and he usually means something nasty.

James G. Huneker (1860-1921)

Wagner's music is better than it sounds.

Mark Twain (1835-1910)

Wagner has beautiful moments but awful quarter hours.

Gioacchino Antonio Rossini (1792-1868)

Wagner is evidently mad.

Hector Berlioz (1803-1869)

Is Wagner a human being at all? Is he not rather a disease?

Friedrich Nietzsche (1844-1900)

I love Wagner, but the music I prefer is that of a cat
hung up by its tail outside a window and trying to
stick to the panes of glass with its claws.

Charles Baudelaire (1821-1867)

Many other musical performances have undergone this
kind of critical analysis, including one noteworthy
amateur recital:

Miss Truman is a unique American phenomenon
with a pleasant voice of little size and fair quality
...yet Miss Truman cannot sing very well. She is
flat a good deal of the time ...she communicates
almost nothing of the music she presents ...There
are few moments during her recital when one can
relax and feel confident that she will make her
goal, which is the end of the song.

Paul Hume
Music critic of the *Washington Post*
On a recital by Margaret Truman 1950

while modern musical forms have hardly been exempt:

Jazz: *Music invented for the torture of imbeciles.*

Henry van Dyke (1852-1933)

I occasionally play works by contemporary com-
posers and for two reasons. First to discourage the
composer from writing any more and secondly to
remind myself how much I appreciate Beethoven.

Jascha Heifetz (b. 1901)

Painters, too, suffered a lack of understanding in their
audience:

A tortoise-shell cat having a fit in a platter of
tomatoes.

Mark Twain (1835-1910)
On a painting by Turner

If the old masters had labeled their fruit, one
wouldn't be so likely to mistake pears for turnips.

Mark Twain (1835-1910)

*If my husband would ever meet a woman on the
street who looked like the women in his paintings,
he would fall over in a dead faint.*

Mrs. Pablo Picasso

and a popular cartoonist adopted a cynical view of
current tendencies in painting:

*Abstract art? A product of the untalented, sold by
the unprincipled to the utterly bewildered.*

Al Capp (b. 1909)

A famous modern sculptor attracted restrained admiration from a cranky modern poet:

*Epstein is a great sculptor. I wish he would wash,
but I believe Michael Angelo never did, so I
suppose it is part of the tradition.*

Ezra Pound (1885-1972)

One of the champions of new forms in both art and
writing was the American author, Gertrude Stein, and
her reception was typical of the reaction to the
contemporary arts:

Gertrude Stein is the mama of dada.

*Miss Stein was a past master in making nothing
happen very slowly.*

Clifton Fadiman (b. 1904)

*There's a wonderful family called Stein,
There's Gert and there's Epp and there's Ein;
Gert's poems are bunk,
Epp's statues are junk,
And no one can understand Ein.*

Anonymous

Those whose ambition is to enrich their conversation
with a higher quality of insult and abuse, those who
aspire to the perfect squelch, have a difficult road to
follow. It is comforting to know that we can always turn
for inspiration to the old standby, Shakespeare, who
seems to have a line for every occasion:

Down, down to hell; and say I sent thee thither.
King Henry VI, Third Part

You blocks, you stones, you worse than senseless things!

The first thing we do, let's kill all the lawyers.

King Henry VI, Second Part

How now, you secret black and midnight hags! What is't you do?

Macbeth

O villain! thou wilt be condemn'd into everlasting redemption for this.

Much Ado About Nothing

Sweep on, you fat and greasy citizens!

Antony and Cleopatra

William Shakespeare (1546-1616)

It is inspiring, too, to realize that although the art of invective has been in a regrettable decline in recent years, a few hardy souls still keep it alive. Regular perusal of the "Letters" column of most newspapers will reveal anonymous artists at work, and give hope for the future:

Sir: During the short time since The Sun *started publishing in Edmonton, I have witnessed your decay from amiable drunk through voyeur and track rat to misogynous, vitriolic pariah.*

... I cannot but from now on dismiss your scribblings as the libelous drivel of an unbalanced mind.

Robert Hamilton

Edmonton Sun 1978

*

The devil damn thee black, thou cream-faced loon!
William Shakespeare (1546-1616)
Macbeth

*

Fatheads! Beanbrains!

Italian proverb

THE UNDISPUTED FAME ENJOYED
BY SHAKESPEARE AS A WRITER ... IS, LIKE
EVERY OTHER LIE,
A GREAT EVIL.

—TOLSTOY

I·WOULD·THE·GODS
HAD·MADE·THEE
MORE·POETICAL·

 *would the gods had made thee more poetical ...*

William Shakespeare (1564-1616)
As You Like It

"Oh, that mine adversary had written a book," lamented Job. Generations of poets, playwrights and novelists since then have learned to their sorrow that the mere act of taking pen to paper leaves a writer open to attack. Literary men and women not only face frontal assault from the critics; they must protect their flanks and rear from the sniping of friends and colleagues. Those who make their living with words seem to be particularly adept at sharpening them as weapons. And perhaps the celebrated artistic temperament is responsible for the remarkably waspish character of a great deal of literary dialogue and the frequency, bitterness and intensity of literary feuds.

Shakespeare has been elevated to a virtually unassailable position among writers of all languages. Yet neither in his own time nor subsequently has the Bard been free from barbs; whether from a green-eyed contemporary —

> *There is an upstart crow beautified with our feathers. That with his tyger's heart wrapt in a player's hide, supposes he is as well able to bombast out a blank verse as the best of you; and being an absolute* Johannes Factotum, *is, in his own conceit, the only Shakescene in a country.*
>
> Robert Greene (1558-1592)

a bored courtier of the Restoration —

> *I saw Hamlet Prince of Denmark, played; but now the old plays begin to disgust this refined age, since his majesty has been so long abroad.*
>
> John Evelyn (1620-1706)

an irreverent monarch —

Was there ever such stuff as great part of Shakes-
peare? only one must not say so! But what think you
— What? Is there not sad stuff? What? — What?
George III (1738-1820)

or an enraged foreigner:

The undisputed fame enjoyed by Shakespeare as a
writer ... is, like every other lie, a great evil.
Count Leo Tolstoy (1828-1910)

The easily pleased Pepys found Shakespeare a bore:

To the King's Theatre, where we saw Midsummer
Night's Dream, *which I had never seen before, nor*
shall ever again, for it is the most insipid, ridiculous
play that ever I saw in my life.
Samuel Pepys (1633-1703)

while a Scottish audience preferred a Scot:

Whaur's yer Wully Shakespeare noo?
Anonymous Scottish theatregoer
On first night of Scottish play *Douglas* 1756

and the Americans were aghast:

Shakespeare, Madam, is obscene, and, thank God,
we are sufficiently advanced to have found it out.
Quoted by Frances Trollope (1780-1863)

But perhaps the most sustained attack on Shakespeare
was mounted by one of his own countrymen, a fellow
playwright. From a perspective of three centuries,
Bernard Shaw took issue with Shakespeare, carrying
away a couple of other public monuments in the process:

With the single exception of Homer, there is no
eminent writer, not even Sir Walter Scott, whom I
can despise so entirely as I despise Shakespeare
when I measure my mind against his. The intensity
of my impatience with him occasionally reaches
such a pitch, that it would positively be a relief to me
to dig him up and throw stones at him, knowing as I

do how incapable he and his worshippers are of understanding any less obvious form of indignity.
Bernard Shaw (1856-1950)
On William Shakespeare

This exercise in provocative journalism brought on the return fire of the faithful:

The way Bernard Shaw believes in himself is very refreshing in these atheistic days when so many people believe in no God at all.
Israel Zangwill (1864-1926)

The theatre itself has endured a siege of insults for nearly two thousand years. From the early Church fathers—

Spending time in the theatres produces fornication, intemperance, and every kind of impurity.
St. John Chrysostom (345?-407)

to turbulent nineteenth-century France—

One should never take one's daughter to a theatre. Not only are plays immoral; the house itself is immoral.
Alexandre Dumas *fils* (1824-1895)

to modern musical comedy—

Don't put your daughter on the stage, Mrs. Worthington!
Noel Coward (1899-1973)

the message has always been the same:

That popular Stage-playes ... are sinfull, heathenish, lewde, ungodly Spectacles, and most pernicious Corruptions; condemned in all ages, as intolerable Mischiefes to Churches, to Republickes, to the manners, mindes and soules of men. And that the Profession of Play-poets, of Stage-players; together with the penning, acting, and frequenting of Stage-playes, are unlawful, infamous and misbeseeming Christians.
William Prynne (1600-1669)

The ire of the early Puritans was particularly violent:

I am persuaded that Satan hath not a more speedy way and fitter school to work and teach his desire, to bring men and women into his share of concupiscence and filthy lusts of wicked whoredom, than those plays and theatres ...

John Northbrooke

Not every condemnation of the theatre has been based on morality. Later commentators were repelled for different reasons:

There is a total extinction of all taste: our authors are vulgar, gross, illiberal; the theatre swarms with wretched translations, and ballad operas, and we have nothing new but improving abuse.

Horace Walpole (1717-1797)

Aside from the moral contamination incident to the average theatre, the influence intellectually is degrading. Its lessons are morbid, distorted, and superficial; they do not mirror life.

T.T. Munger

Is it a stale remark to say that I have constantly found the interest excited at a playhouse to bear an exact inverse proportion to the price paid for admission?

Charles Lamb (1775-1834)

English plays,
Atrocious in content,
Absurd in form,
Objectionable in action,
Execrable English theatre!

Johann Wolfgang von Goethe (1749-1832)

But a sage of the enlightenment took just the opposite view:

Whoever condemns the theatre is an enemy to his country.

Voltaire (1694-1778)

Poetry, too, has been a ripe field for the caustic critic.

47

John Milton, the great seventeenth-century poet, met with a certain lack of enthusiasm on literary grounds:

Our language sunk under him.

Joseph Addison (1672-1719)
On John Milton

Paradise Lost *is one of the books which the reader admires and lays down, and forgets to take up again. Its perusal is a duty rather than a pleasure.*

Samuel Johnson (1709-1784)

This obscure, eccentric and disgusting poem.

Voltaire (1694-1778)

But it was his political involvement that provoked the lowest blow (the poet had recently lost his sight):

Having never had any mental vision, he has now lost his bodily sight; a silly coxcomb, fancifying himself a beauty; an unclean beast, with nothing more human about him than his guttering eyelids; the fittest doom for him would be to hang him on the highest gallows, and set his head on the Tower of London.

Salmasius (Claude de Saumaise) (1588-1653)
On John Milton

The late seventeenth century was the age of poetic satire, and many a heroic couplet laid bare the deficiencies of the author's literary rivals. The leading exponent of this sort of verse was the malicious and venomous Alexander Pope, whose tiny stature, low origins and verbal sting earned him the nickname "the wicked wasp of Twickenham":

The verses, when they were written, resembled nothing so much as spoonfuls of boiling oil, ladled out by a fiendish monkey at an upstairs window upon such of the passers-by whom the wretch had a grudge against.

Lytton Strachey (1880-1932)
On Alexander Pope

Pope's boiling oil scalded a wide variety of victims, most of high estate—

Yet let me flap this bug with gilded wings,
This painted child of dirt, that stinks and stings ...
Alexander Pope (1688-1744)
On Lord Hervey

His passion still, to covet general praise,
His life, to forfeit it a thousand ways.
Alexander Pope (1688-1744)
On Lord Wharton

some of low—as in these verses written for the collar of the Prince Regent's pet dog:

I am His Highness' dog at Kew;
Pray tell me, sir, whose dog are you?
Alexander Pope (1688-1744)

He clearly relished the deference won by his scathing tongue:

Yes, I am proud; and must be proud, to see
Men not afraid of God afraid of me.
Alexander Pope (1688-1744)

—a jibe which gave one of the wounded a chance to get a little of his own back:

The great honour of that boast is such
That hornets and mad dogs may boast as much.
Lord Hervey (1696-1743)
On Alexander Pope

Prose writers, no less than poets and dramatists, took full part in the literary fray:

Now, it must be understood that ink is the great missive weapon in all battles of the learned, which, conveyed through a sort of engine called a quill, infinite numbers of these are darted at the enemy by the valiant on both sides, with equal skill and violence, as if it were an engagement of porcupines.
Jonathan Swift (1667-1745)

Swift knew whereof he spoke. Some quills he darted himself:

I cannot but conclude the bulk of your natives to be

49

the most pernicious race of little odious vermin that nature ever suffered to crawl upon the surface of the earth.

Jonathan Swift (1667-1745)
Gulliver's Travels

and others were launched in his direction:

A monster gibbering shrieks, and gnashing imprecations against mankind — tearing down all shreds of modesty, past all sense of manliness and shame; filthy in word, filthy in thought, furious, raging, obscene.

William Makepeace Thackeray (1811-1863)
On Jonathan Swift

The towering literary figure of the late eighteenth century was Dr. Samuel Johnson — literary critic, compiler of the famous dictionary, but above all, a brilliant and formidable conversationalist. The age demanded slashing and often rude repartee, and the gruff, bearlike Johnson was a master of the verbal put-down — the more because he knew it was expected of him. Recorded by the omnipresent James Boswell, by Fanny Kemble and Mrs. Thrale, many of Johnson's sallies retain their vigor even today.

The good doctor had outspoken opinions on many of his contemporaries and on an inexhaustible variety of other subjects:

Mrs. Montagu has dropt me. Now Sir, there are people whom one should like very well to drop, but would not wish to be dropt by.
*
Sir, I never did the man an injury; yet he would read his tragedy to me.
*
Sir, there is no settling the precedency between a louse and a flea.

> On being asked whether Herrick or
> Smart was the better poet

*
Sir, he was dull in company, dull in his closet, dull everywhere. He was dull in a new way, and that made many people think him GREAT. He was a mechanical poet.

> On Thomas Gray

*
He hardly drank tea without a strategem.

> On Alexander Pope

*
Why, Sir, Sherry is dull, naturally dull; but it must have taken him a great deal of pains to become what we now see him. Such excess of stupidity, Sir, is not in nature.

> On Thomas Sheridan

*
The misfortune of Goldsmith in conversation is this: he goes on without knowing how he is to get off.

> On Oliver Goldsmith

*
No man will be a sailor who has contrivance enough to get himself into a jail; for being in a ship is being in a jail, with the chance of being drowned. A man in jail has more room, better food, and commonly better company.
*
PATRON: n.s. One who countenances, supports or protects. Commonly a wretch who supports with insolence, and is paid with flattery.

> Samuel Johnson (1709-1784)

Not everyone admired Johnson's style —

Johnson made the most brutal speeches to living persons; for though he was good-natured at bottom, he was ill-natured at top. He loved to dispute to show his superiority. If his opponents were weak, he told them they were fools; if they vanquished him, he was scurrilous.

Horace Walpole (1717-1797)

Casts of manure a wagon-load around
To raise a simple daisy from the ground;
Uplifts the club of Hercules, for what?
To crush a butterfly or brain a gnat!

John Wolcot (1738-1819)
On Samuel Johnson

or, for that matter, Boswell's:

Have you got Boswell's most absurd enormous book? — the best thing in it is a bon mot of Lord Pembroke. The more one learns of Johnson, the more preposterous assemblage he appears of strong sense, of the lowest bigotry and prejudices, of pride, brutality, fretfulness and vanity — and Boswell is the ape of most of his faults, without a grain of his sense. It is the story of a mountebank and his zany.

Horace Walpole (1717-1797)

Sir, you have but two topics, yourself and me. I am sick of both.

Samuel Johnson (1709-1784)
To James Boswell

Johnson's definition of a patron may have been tempered by his experience with Lord Chesterfield. He had appealed to Chesterfield for his patronage during the preparation of the Dictionary, but the nobleman made no helpful move until, ten hard years later, when the great work was ready for publication, he wrote two supporting articles. Enraged at Chesterfield's opportunism, Johnson sent him a classical and icy rebuke:

Is not a patron, my lord, one who looks with unconcern on a man struggling for life in the water, and when he has reached ground encumbers him with help? The notice which you have been pleased to take of my labours, had it been early, had been kind; but it has been delayed until I am indifferent, and cannot enjoy it; till I am known, and do not want it.

I hope it is no very cynical asperity not to confess obligations where no benefit has been received, or to be unwilling that the public should consider me as owing that to a patron which Providence has enabled me to do for myself. Having carried on my work thus far with so little obligation to any favourer of learning, I shall not be disappointed though I should conclude it, if less be possible, with less; for I have been long wakened from that dream of hope, in which I once boasted myself with so much exultation, my lord — Your lordship's most humble, most obedient servant,

Sam. Johnson

Samuel Johnson (1709-1784)
To Lord Chesterfield

When Chesterfield's letters of advice to his son were published, Johnson observed:

They inculcate the morals of a whore, and the manners of a dancing master.

Samuel Johnson (1709-1784)

One of the sensations of the day was James MacPherson's "translation" of an obscure Scottish epic poem. When Johnson denounced "Ossian" as a forgery, MacPherson challenged him to a duel. The doctor sent a peremptory reply:

Mr. James MacPherson — I received your foolish and impudent letter. Any violence offered me I shall do my best to repel; and what I cannot do for myself, the law shall do for me. I hope I shall never be deterred from detecting what I think to be a cheat, by the menaces of a ruffian.

What would you have me retract? I thought your book an imposture; I think it an imposture still. For this opinion I have given my reasons to the publick which I here dare you to refute. Your rage I defy. Your abilities ... are not so formidable; and what I hear of your morals, inclines me to pay regard not to what you shall say, but to what you shall prove. You may print this if you will.

Sam. Johnson.

Samuel Johnson (1709-1784)

When Johnson died he was memorialized by his contemporaries in epitaphs that were less than charitable:

Here lies Sam Johnson: —Reader, have a care,
Tread lightly, lest you wake a sleeping bear:
Religious, moral, generous and humane
He was: but self-sufficient, proud, and vain.
Fond of, and overbearing in, dispute,
A Christian and a scholar — but a brute.

Soame Jenyns (1704-1787)
On Samuel Johnson

Another superb conversationalist whose life spanned the eighteenth and nineteenth centuries was the Reverend Sidney Smith, sometime Canon of St. Paul's Cathedral. Smith's attitude to the world was one of amused tolerance. More urbane and less pompous than Johnson, he used the needle rather than the club:

No one minds what Jeffrey says. ... It's not more than a week ago that I heard him speak disrespectfully of the Equator.

I have to believe in the Apostolic Succession. There is no other way of explaining the descent of the Bishop of Exeter from Judas Iscariot.

He has spent all his life in letting down empty buckets into empty wells; and he is frittering away his age in trying to draw them up again.

Sidney Smith (1771-1845)

When Lord Brougham, a lawyer with an unsavoury

reputation, arrived at the theatre during a performance of *The Messiah,* Smith announced:

Here comes counsel for the other side.

Sidney Smith (1771-1845)
On Lord Brougham

Smith's droll wit encompassed subjects as diverse as music —

Nothing can be more disgusting than Oratorio. How absurd, to see five hundred people fiddling like madmen about the Israelites in the Red Sea!

country living —

I have no relish for the country. It is a kind of healthy grave.

and the Church —

There are three sexes — men, women and clergymen.

Sidney Smith (1771-1845)

When it was proposed that St. Paul's be surrounded by a wooden sidewalk, Smith agreed:

Let the Dean and Canons lay their heads together and the thing will be done.

Sidney Smith (1771-1845)

Many of his jibes were at his own expense:

When I am in the pulpit, I have the pleasure of seeing my audience nod approbation while they sleep.
*
You and I are exceptions to the laws of nature; you have risen by your gravity, and I have sunk by my levity.

Sidney Smith (1771-1845)

The ironic Smith tone of voice is at its best in this civilized note to Lord John Russell:

You say you are not convinced by my pamphlet. I

am afraid that I am a very arrogant person, but I do assure you, that in the fondest moments of self-conceit, the idea of convincing a Russell that he was wrong never came across my mind. Euclid would have had a bad chance with you if you had happened to have formed an opinion that the interior angles of a triangle were not equal to two right angles. The more poor Euclid demonstrated, the more you would not have been convinced.

Sydney Smith (1771-1845)
To Lord John Russell

A favorite target of Smith and many others was the brilliant but ponderous Thomas Babington Macaulay. Macaulay was a nonstop talker, and his friends despaired of getting a word in edgewise:

You know, when I am gone you will be sorry you never heard me speak.

Sydney Smith (1771-1845)
To Thomas Babington Macaulay

Macaulay is laying waste society with his water-spouts of talk; people in his company burst for want of an opportunity of dropping in a word.

Henry Reeve
On Thomas Babington Macaulay

Macaulay is well for a while, but one wouldn't live under Niagara.

Thomas Carlyle (1795-1881)
On Thomas Babington Macaulay

Macaulay is like a book in breeches ... he has occasional flashes of silence that make his conversation perfectly delightful.

Sydney Smith (1771-1845)
On Thomas Babington Macaulay

Macaulay read omniverously almost from the time he could walk. He never forgot a thing—

He could repeat the whole History of the Virtuous Blue-Coat Boy in 3 volumes, post 8vo, without a slip.

He should take two tablespoonfuls of the waters of Lethe every morning.

Sidney Smith (1771-1845)
On Thomas Babington Macaulay

and he was only too prepared to share his awesome knowledge with others:

I wish I was as cocksure of anything as Tom Macaulay is of everything.

Viscount Melbourne (1770-1848)

He not only overflowed with learning, but stood in the slop.

Sidney Smith (1771-1845)
On Thomas Babington Macaulay

As an essayist and literary critic, as well as a lawyer, politician and administrator, Macaulay had frequent opportunities to launch thunderbolts of his own:

His imagination resembled the wings of an ostrich. It enabled him to run, though not to soar.

Thomas Babington Macaulay (1800-1859)

Macaulay took a dim view of British hypocrisy:

The Puritan hated bear-baiting, not because it gave pain to the bear, but because it gave pleasure to the spectators.

We know no spectacle so ridiculous as the British public in one of its periodical fits of morality.

Thomas Babington Macaulay (1800-1859)

He was not a fan of James Boswell, the chronicler of Johnson:

Servile and impertinent, shallow and pedantic, a bigot and a sot, bloated with family pride, and eternally blustering about the dignity of a born gentleman, yet stooping to be a talebearer, an eavesdropper, a common butt in the taverns of London. ... Everything which another man would have hidden, everything the publication of which would have made another man hang himself, was

57

matter of exaltation to his weak and diseased mind.
Thomas Babington Macaulay (1800-1859)
On James Boswell

But it was in his review of the memoirs of the French revolutionary, Bertrand Barère, that Macaulay achieved what has been described, with only slight exaggeration, as "the most sustained piece of invective in the English language."

> *... Our opinion then is this: that Barère approached nearer than any person mentioned in history or fiction, whether man or devil, to the idea of consummate and universal depravity. In him the qualities which are the proper objects of contempt, preserve an exquisite and absolute harmony. When we put everything together, sensuality, poltroonery, baseness, effrontery, mendacity, barbarity, the result is something which in a novel we should condemn as caricature, and to which, we venture to say, no parallel can be found in history.*

> *... A man who has never been within the tropics does not know what a thunderstorm means; a man who has never looked on Niagara has but a faint idea of a cataract; and he who has not read Barère's* Memoirs *may be said not to know what it is to lie.*
> Thomas Babington Macaulay (1800-1859)
> On Bertrand Barère

For all Macaulay's ability, there were those who did not think much of him:

> *At bottom, this Macaulay is but a poor creature with his dictionary literature and erudition, his saloon arrogance. He has no vision in him. He will neither see nor do any great thing.*
> Thomas Carlyle (1795-1881)
> On Thomas Babington Macaulay

The power of the press was beginning to make itself felt, and personal attack was the vogue. The anonymous letters of "Junius" appeared in the popular *Public*

Advertiser, and one of them disembowelled the descendant of an illegitimate son of Charles II:

> *It is not that you do wrong by design, but that you should never do right by mistake. It is not that your indolence and your activity have been equally misapplied, but that the first uniform principle or ... genius of your life, should have carried you through every possible change and contradiction of conduct without the momentary imputation or colour of a virtue; and that the wildest spirit of inconsistency should never once have betrayed you into a wise or honourable action ...*

> *You may look back with pleasure to an illustrious pedigree in which heraldry has not left a single good quality upon record to insult or upbraid you. ... Charles the First lived and died a hypocrite. Charles the Second was a hypocrite of another sort, and should have died upon the same scaffold. At the distance of a century, we see their different characters happily revived, and blended in your Grace. Sullen and severe without religion, profligate without gaiety, you live like Charles the Second, without being an amiable companion, and, for aught I know, may die as his father did, without the reputation of a martyr.*

"Junius"
Letter to the Duke of Grafton 1769

The early nineteenth century saw the dawn of the Romantic Age, and it brought a series of fierce literary skirmishes. The Romantic poets were a wild and prickly group, viewed by many as barbarians. When they were not firing back at their critics, they trained their sights on one another.

The consumptive John Keats was the first conspicuous victim. His lush verses were, it seems, little appreciated by at least one of his fellow poets:

> *Here are Jonny Keats' piss-a-bed poetry, and three novels by God knows whom. ... No more Keats, I*

entreat: flay him alive; if some of you don't I must skin him myself: there is no bearing the drivelling idiotism of the Mankin.

Lord Byron (1788-1824)

Keats's work was savagely attacked by the fashionable literary magazines, the *Quarterly Review* and *Blackwood's:*

The Phrenzy of the "Poems" was bad enough in its way; but it did not alarm us half so seriously as the calm, settled, imperturbable drivelling idiocy of "Endymion." ... Mr. Hunt is a small poet, but he is a clever man. Mr. Keats is a still smaller poet, and he is only a boy of pretty abilities, which he has done everything in his power to spoil ... We venture to make one small prophecy, that his bookseller will not a second time venture £50 upon any thing he can write. It is a better and a wiser thing to be a starved apothecary than a starved poet; so back to the shop, Mr. John, back to "plasters, pills, and ointment boxes," etc.

Blackwood's Magazine
On John Keats 1818

JOHN KEATS

Keats promptly died, and his friend and champion Shelley promoted the notion that he had been mortally wounded by his bad reviews:

> *It may be well said that these wretched men know not what they do. . . . What gnat did they strain at here, after having swallowed all those camels? Against what women taken in adultery dares the foremost of these literary prostitutes to cast his opprobrious stone? Miserable man! You, one of the meanest, have wantonly defaced one of the noblest specimens of the workmanship of God. Nor shall it be your excuse that, murderer as you are, you have spoken daggers, but used none.*
>
> Percy Bysshe Shelley (1792-1822)
> *Preface to "Adonais"*

Even Byron had a partial change of heart and weighed in against the critics:

> *Who killed John Keats?*
> *"I", says the Quarterly,*
> *So savage and Tartarly;*
> *"'Twas one of my feats."*
>
> Lord Byron (1788-1824)

But the class-conscious reviewers were unrepentant and their opinion was later shared by Thomas Carlyle, surveying a biography of Keats:

> *Fricassee of dead dog. . . . A truly unwise little book. The kind of man that Keats was gets ever more horrible to me. Force of hunger for pleasure of every kind, and want of all other force — such a soul, it would once have been very evident, was a chosen "vessel of Hell".*
>
> Thomas Carlyle (1795-1881)
> On Monckton Milnes's *Life of Keats*

Shelley, of course, had good reason to resent the literary reviews. The *Quarterly* had been particularly unkind to him:

> *Mr. Shelley is a very vain man; and like most vain*

men, he is but half instructed in knowledge and less than half disciplined in reasoning powers; his vanity ... has been his ruin.

Quarterly Review
On Percy Bysshe Shelley 1817

But then, so had some of his fellows:

Shelley is a poor creature, who has said or done nothing worth a serious man being at the trouble of remembering. ... Poor soul, he has always seemed to me an extremely weak creature; a poor, thin, spasmodic, hectic shrill and pallid being. ... The very voice of him, shrill, shrieky, to my ear has too much of the ghost.

Thomas Carlyle (1795-1881)
On Percy Bysshe Shelley

He was a liar and a cheat; he paid no regard to truth, nor to any kind of moral obligation.

Robert Southey (1774-1843)
On Percy Bysshe Shelley

A lewd vegetarian.

Charles Kingsley (1819-1875)
On Percy Bysshe Shelley

Byron's spectacular social life led many to take a skeptical view of him:

The most affected of sensualists and the most pretentious of profligates.

Algernon Swinburne (1837-1909)
On Lord Byron

A denaturalized being who, having exhausted every species of sensual gratification, and drained the cup of sin to its bitterest dregs, is resolved to show that he is no longer human, even in his frailties, but a cool, unconcerned fiend.

John Styles
On Lord Byron

but he retaliated with a sharp pen. He did not, it appears, think highly of many of his peers:

*I have no patience with the sort of trash you send me
out by way of books ... I never saw such work or
works. Campbell is lecturing — Moore idling —
Southey twaddling — Wordsworth drivelling —
Coleridge muddling — Joanna Baillie piddling —
Bowles quibbling, squabbling, and snivelling.*

Lord Byron (1788-1824)

*Let simple Wordsworth chime his childish verse,
And brother Coleridge lull the babe at nurse.*

Lord Byron (1788-1824)

Byron didn't mind stooping to attack; he once serenaded
an unfortunately named poet laureate:

*Oh, Amos Cottle — Phoebus, what a name
To fill the speaking trump of future fame!
Oh, Amos Cottle, for a moment think
What meagre profits spring from pen and ink!*

Lord Byron (1788-1824)

Like many of the other Romantics, Byron died young; had
he lived, we might never have heard his name:

*Byron! — he would be all forgotten today if he had
lived to be a florid old gentleman with iron-grey
whiskers, writing very long, very able letters to* The
Times *about the Repeal of the Corn Laws.*

Max Beerbohm (1872-1956)

63

One poetic young Turk who did achieve Establishment respectability was William Wordsworth, reaching dubious heights as poet laureate.

> *In his youth, Wordsworth sympathized with the French Revolution, went to France, wrote good poetry, and had a natural daughter. At this period, he was a "bad" man.*
>
> *Then he became "good", abandoned his daughter, adopted correct principles, and wrote bad poetry.*
> Bertrand Russell (1872-1970)

> *Just for a handful of silver he left us,*
> *Just for a riband to stick in his coat.*
> Robert Browning (1812-1889)
> *The Lost Leader*

It was partly Wordsworth's poetry that upset his critics—

> *Dank, limber verses, stuft with lakeside sedges,*
> *And propt with rotten stakes from rotten hedges.*
> Walter Savage Landor (1775-1864)

> *Two voices are there: one is of the deep;*
> *It learns the storm-cloud's thunderous melody ...*
> *And one is of an old half-witted sheep*
> *Which bleats articulate monotony ...*
> *And, Wordsworth, both are thine.*
> James Kenneth Stephen (1859-1892)

> *Is Wordsworth a bell with a wooden tongue?*
> Ralph Waldo Emerson (1803-1882)

> *Who both by precept and example shows*
> *That prose is verse, and verse is merely prose.*
> Lord Byron (1788-1824)

and partly his personality—

> *Wordsworth has left a bad impression wherever he visited in town by his egotism, vanity and bigotry.*
> John Keats (1795-1821)

64

For prolixity, thinness, endless dilution, it excels all
the other speech I had heard from mortals. . . . The
languid way in which he gives you a handful of
numb unresponsive fingers is very significant.

Thomas Carlyle (1795-1881)
On William Wordsworth

The moral repression of the nineteenth century seems
only to have egged on the outspoken; literary infighting
took place in the foothills as well as on the mountain
peaks.

The essayist William Hazlitt also wrote for the
Edinburgh Review, so he was on both sides of the
author-critic controversy. His friends took mild exception to his critiques:

In God's name, why could you not tell Mr. Shelley
in a pleasant manner of what you dislike in him?
. . . How do you think that friends can eternally
live upon their good behaviour in this way, and be
cordial and comfortable or whatever else you
choose they should be—for it is difficult to find
out—on pain of being drawn and quartered in
your paragraphs.

Leigh Hunt (1784-1859)
To William Hazlitt

while other observers were more forthright:

He abuses all poets, with the single exception of
Milton; he abuses all country-people; he abuses the
English; he abuses the Irish; he abuses the Scotch.
. . . if the creature . . . must make his way over the
tombs of illustrious men, disfiguring the records of
their greatness with the slime and filth which
marks his track, it is right to point him out, that he
may be flung back to the situation in which nature
designed that he should grovel.

Quarterly Review
On William Hazlitt 1817

A mere ulcer; a sore from head to foot; a poor devil

*so completely flayed that there is not a square inch
of healthy flesh on his carcass; an overgrown pimple, sore to the touch.*

Quarterly Review
On William Hazlitt 1817

Celebrated persons even considered him socially
unacceptable:

His manners are 99 in a 100 singularly repulsive.

Samuel Taylor Coleridge (1772-1834)

and took their revenge by writing unpleasant little
epitaphs:

*Under this stone does William Hazlitt lie
Thankless of all that God or man could give,
He lived like one who never thought to die,
He died like one who dared not hope to live.*

Samuel Taylor Coleridge (1772-1834)

The growing savagery of the literary critics provoked
the Gaelic wrath of even so amiable a poet as Robert
Burns:

*Thou eunuch of language ... thou pimp of gender
... murderous accoucheur of infant learning
... thou pickle-herring in the puppet show of
nonsense.*

Robert Burns (1759-1796)
On an anonymous critic

If this seems excessive, it was merely the latest volley
in a long war. A sixteenth-century Frenchman
expressed the views of authors of all ages:

*As for you, little envious Prigs, snarling, bastard,
puny Criticks, you'll soon have railed your last: Go
hang yourselves.*

François Rabelais (c. 1490-1553)

In his wake followed a host of others:

*They who write ill, and they who ne'er durst write,
Turn critics out of mere revenge and spite.*

John Dryden (1631-1700)

The critic's symbol should be the tumble-bug; he deposits his egg in somebody else's dung, otherwise he could not hatch it.

Mark Twain (1835-1910)

A louse in the locks of literature.

Alfred, Lord Tennyson (1809-1894)
On critic Churton Collins

and many successors, including angry fathers, have kept the tradition alive:

I have just read your lousy review buried in the back pages. You sound like a frustrated old man who never made a success, an eight-ulcer man on a four-ulcer job, and all four ulcers working. I have never met you, but if I do you'll need a new nose and plenty of beefsteak and perhaps a supporter below.

Harry S Truman (1884-1972)
To *Washington Post* music critic Paul Hume

The verbal jousting of the Romantics merely set the stage for what was to follow. The writers of the later nineteenth century displayed an extraordinary ingenuity in personal abuse.

Leading the field as a one-man demolition squad was the cantankerous Thomas Carlyle, who, afflicted by chronic dyspepsia, suffered fools not gladly and his fellow writers hardly at all:

Charles Lamb I sincerely believe to be in some considerable degree insane. A more pitiful, rickety, gasping, staggering, stammering Tomfool I do not know.

On Charles Lamb

A weak, diffusive, weltering, ineffectual man. ... Never did I see such apparatus got ready for thinking, and so little thought. He mounts scaffolding, pulleys and tackle, gathers all the tools in the neighbourhood with labour, with noise, demonstration, precept, abuse, and sets — three bricks.

On Coleridge

Gladstone appears to me one of the contemptiblest

men I ever looked on. A poor Ritualist; almost
spectral kind of phantasm of a man ...

On William Ewart Gladstone

The most unending ass in Christendom.

On Herbert Spencer

I have no patience whatever with these gorilla
damnifications of humanity.

On Charles Darwin

Thomas Carlyle (1795-1881)

Carlyle once refused to receive the poet Swinburne, on the
grounds that he had no wish to meet someone who was

sitting in a sewer, and adding to it.

In Swinburne, Carlyle met his match, for if anyone could
be more vitriolic than the Scot it was this effete young
man caricatured as the "fleshly poet" in Gilbert and
Sullivan's *Patience.* Swinburne deplored

the immaculate Calvinism of so fiery and so forcible
a champion of slave-holding and slave-torture as
Mr. Carlyle.

Algernon Swinburne (1837-1909)

and extended the compliment to the rest of the family —

That very sorry pair of phenomena, Thomas Cloacina and his Goody.

Algernon Swinburne (1837-1909)
On the Carlyles

a sentiment shared by others:

It was very good of God to let Carlyle and Mrs. Carlyle marry one another and so make only two people miserable instead of four.

Samuel Butler (1835-1902)

His own poetry was under sustained attack for its supposed immorality (*Punch* called him "*Swine*-born"):

I attempt to describe Mr. Swinburne; and lo! the Bacchanal screams, the sterile Dolores sweats, serpents dance, men and women wrench, wriggle, and foam in an endless alliteration of heated and meaningless words ...

Robert Buchanan (1841-1901)
On Algernon Swinburne

But Swinburne was himself enraged by what he saw as a lack of morality in others. The American poet, Walt Whitman, especially offended him:

Under the dirty clumsy paws of a harper whose plectrum is a muck-rake, any tune will become a chaos of dischords. ... Mr. Whitman's Eve is a drunken apple-woman, indecently sprawling in the slush and garbage of the gutter amid the rotten refuse of her overturned fruit-stall: but Mr. Whitman's Venus is a Hottentot wench under the influence of cantharides and adulterated rum.

Algernon Swinburne (1837-1909)
On Walt Whitman

and even the good grey Tennyson was suspect:

The Vivien of Mr. Tennyson's idyll seems to me ... about the most base and repulsive person ever set forth in serious literature. Her impurity is actually eclipsed by her incredible and incomparable vulgar-

ity. ... She is such a sordid creature as plucks men passing by the sleeve. ... The conversation of Vivien is exactly described in the poet's own phrase — it is "as the poached filth that floods the middle street."

Algernon Swinburne (1837-1909)
On Alfred, Lord Tennyson

(Tennyson, on reading his poem *Lucretius* to a friend, was said to remark:

What a mess little Swinburne would have made of this.)

One of Swinburne's most famous run-ins was with the "Sage of Concord," Ralph Waldo Emerson. He had read in an American paper that Emerson had described him as

a perfect leper, and a mere sodomite.

and had promptly dispatched a polite commentary:

I am informed that certain American journalists, not content with providing filth of their own for the consumption of their kind, sometimes offer to their readers a dish of beastliness which they profess to have gathered from under the chairs of more distinguished men.

I ... am not sufficiently expert in the dialect of the cesspool and the dung-cart to retort in their own kind on these venerable gentlemen — I, whose ears and lips alike are unused to the amenities of conversation embroidered with such fragments of flowery rhetoric as may be fished up by congenial fingers or lapped up by congenial tongues out of the sewage of Sodom. ...

[These are] the last tricks of tongue now possible to a gap-toothed and hoary-headed ape, ... who now in his dotage spits and chatters from a dirtier perch of his own finding and fouling ...

Algernon Swinburne (1837-1909)
To Ralph Waldo Emerson

The pained Emerson made no reply. Swinburne fired off another letter, in much the same terms; but the correspondence did not flourish—perhaps because

> *Emerson is one who lives instinctively on ambrosia—and leaves everything indigestible on his plate.*
>
> Friedrich Nietzsche (1844-1900)
> On Ralph Waldo Emerson

> *I could readily see in Emerson ...a gaping flaw. It was the insinuation that had he lived in those days when the world was made, he might have offered some valuable suggestions.*
>
> Herman Melville (1819-1891)
> On Ralph Waldo Emerson

The general reaction to modern literature was summed up by one disapproving onlooker:

> *Great literature is the creation, for the most part, of disreputable characters, many of whom looked rather seedy, some of whom were drunken blackguards, a few of whom were swindlers or perpetual borrowers, rowdies, gamblers or slaves to a drug.*
>
> Alexander Harvey

That Charles Dickens, then at the height of his powers as a writer, had a good ear for the language of invective is clear from many satirical passages in his novels— particularly *The Pickwick Papers.* Occasionally he employed this talent in earnest:

> *In the foreground of the carpenter's shop is a hideous, wry-necked, blubbering, red-haired boy in a nightgown, who appears to have received a poke playing in an adjacent gutter, and to be holding it up for the contemplation of a kneeling woman, so horrible in her ugliness that (supposing it were possible for any human creature to exist for a*

moment with that dislocated throat) she would
stand out from the rest of the company as a monster
in the vilest cabaret in France or the lowest gin-shop
in England.

Charles Dickens (1812-1870)
On Millais's "Christ in the House of His Parents"

Another figure around whom controversy swirled was
James McNeill Whistler, the expatriate American artist
and notable dandy, who was a champion of the new "art
for art's sake" painters and writers. One of the first to
tangle with Whistler was John Ruskin, the fiercely
moralistic essayist and art critic:

> *Ruskin is one of the most turbid and fallacious*
> *minds ... of the century. To the service of the most*
> *wildly eccentric thoughts he brings the acerbity of a*
> *bigot. ... His mental temperament is that of the*
> *first Spanish Grand Inquisitor. He is a Torquemada*
> *of aesthetics. ... He would burn alive the critic who*
> *disagrees with him. ... Since stakes do not stand*
> *within his reach, he can at least rave and rage in*
> *word, and annihilate the heretic figuratively by*
> *abuse and cursing.*

Max Nordau (1849-1923)
On John Ruskin

Ruskin had little use for the painting of his day,
especially that of the new school:

> *I never saw anything so impudent on the walls of*
> *any exhibition, in any country, as last year in*
> *London. It was a daub professing to be a "harmony*
> *in pink and white" (or some such nonsense);*
> *absolute rubbish, and which had taken about a*
> *quarter of an hour to scrawl or daub — it had no*
> *pretence to be called painting. The price asked for it*
> *was two hundred and fifty guineas.*

John Ruskin (1819-1900)
On Whistler's "Symphony in Grey and Green"

Offended by Whistler's exotic life-style and "frivolous"
painting, Ruskin continued to belabor him:

I have seen and heard much of cockney impudence
before now; but never expected to hear a coxcomb
ask two hundred guineas for flinging a pot of paint
in the public's face.

John Ruskin (1819-1900)
On Whistler's "The Falling Rocket"

The thin-skinned Whistler promptly sued Ruskin for libel; he won his case, but the jury, art critics themselves no doubt, would award him only a farthing in damages!

An early disciple of Whistler was Oscar Wilde, then building his reputation as a conversational lion.

WILDE: (after a bright remark by Whistler) I wish I had said that!
WHISTLER: You will, Oscar, you will!

Whistler (with good reason) accused Wilde of plagiarism, and the ensuing skirmish was conducted, to universal amusement, in the editorial pages of the London papers:

Sir: What has Oscar in common with Art? except that he dines at our tables and picks from our platters the plums for the pudding he peddles in the provinces. Oscar — the amiable, irresponsible, esurient Oscar — with no more sense of a picture than the fit of a coat, has the courage of the opinions ... of others!

James McNeill Whistler (1834-1903)
The World 1886

Sir: ... As Mr. James Whistler has had the impertinence to attack me with both venom and vulgarity in your columns, I hope you will allow me to state that the assertions contained in his letters are as deliberately untrue as they are deliberately offensive.

As for borrowing Mr. Whistler's ideas about art, the only thoroughly original ideas I have ever heard him express have had reference to his own superiority as a painter over painters greater than himself.

Oscar Wilde (1854-1900)
Truth 1890

OSCAR FINGAL
O'FLAHERTIE WILLS
WILDE c. 1882
IN AMERICA

Whistler finally withdrew from the fray:

I'm lonesome. They are all dying. I have hardly a warm personal enemy left.

James McNeill Whistler (1834-1903)

The polished, sophisticated conversation of Oscar Wilde raised the put-down to a different level. As the nineteenth century drew to a close, his huge success marked a significant change in direction for literary insult. Gradually it has become more detached, less filled with personal venom. Epigrammatic and cynical, Wilde's verbal thrusts were a wry commentary on life, but were basically too good-natured to qualify as invective. He relied heavily on turning the expectations of his listeners upside-down:

He is old enough to know worse.
*
One of those characteristic British faces that, once seen, are never remembered.
*
A cynic is a man who knows the price of everything and the value of nothing.
*
The English public takes no interest in a work of art until it is told that the work in question is immoral.

Oscar Wilde (1854-1900)

Wilde's quips were often personal, but were contrived more for their effect on the audience than on the victim:

Henry James writes fiction as if it were a painful duty.
*
The gods have bestowed on Max the gift of perpetual old age.
            On Max Beerbohm
*
George Moore wrote brilliant English until he discovered grammar.
*
There are two ways of disliking poetry: one way is to dislike it, the other is to read Pope.
*
Bernard Shaw is an excellent man; he has not an enemy in the world, and none of his friends like him.

The first rule for a young playwright to follow is not to write like Henry Arthur Jones. ... The second and third rules are the same.

Oscar Wilde (1854-1900)

Frank Harris was to become Wilde's biographer:

Frank Harris is invited to all the great houses in England — once.

*
Every great man nowadays has his disciples, and it is always Judas who writes the biography.

Oscar Wilde (1854-1900)

Although he was constantly embroiled in it, Wilde shrank from controversy:

I dislike arguments of any kind. They are always vulgar, and often convincing.

Nor did he admire the literary lions of the day:

One must have a heart of stone to read the death of little Nell without laughing.

On Dickens's *Old Curiosity Shop*

Even at his lowest moment Wilde was able to muster a *bon mot*. Handcuffed, standing in a pouring rain on his way to prison, Oscar remarked:

If this is the way Queen Victoria treats her convicts, she doesn't deserve to have any.

Oscar Wilde (1854-1900)

Meanwhile, across the Atlantic, another brilliant writer and sardonic observer of the human condition was delighting audiences with his wry wit.

He could charm an audience an hour on a stretch without ever getting rid of an idea.

Mark Twain (1835-1910)

Mark Twain was a genuinely funny man, but a vein of pessimism was never far beneath the surface. His lectures were laced with quips and comments that reflected unfavorably on his fellow man.

When some men discharge an obligation, you can hear the report for miles around.

I am not an editor of a newspaper and shall always try to do right and be good so that God will not make me one.

Man is the only animal that blushes. Or needs to.

Such is the human race. Often it does seem a pity that Noah and his party didn't miss the boat.

Mark Twain (1835-1910)

He tended to take a dim view of officialdom in all its guises:

Fleas can be taught nearly anything that a Congressman can.

It could probably be shown by facts and figures that there is no distinctively native American criminal class except Congress.

In the first place God made idiots; this was for practice; then he made school boards.

Mark Twain (1835-1910)

His admiration for one of the great Empire-builders was not unmixed:

> *I admire him, I frankly confess it; and when his time comes I shall buy a piece of the rope for a keepsake.*
>
> Mark Twain (1835-1910)
> On Cecil Rhodes

Mark Twain had an easily roused temper, and he carried on his campaign against bureaucracy into his private life:

> *Some day you will move me almost to the verge of irritation by your chuckle-headed Goddamned fashion of shutting your Goddamned gas off without giving any notice to your Goddamned parishioners. Several times you have come within an ace of smothering half of this household in their beds and blowing up the other half by this idiotic, not to say criminal, custom of yours. And it has happened again today. Haven't you a telephone?*
>
> Mark Twain (1835-1910)
> Letter to the Gas Company

Yet his sense of humor was irrepressible; the spirit of the man is demonstrated in the joke he played on his close friend, William Howells:

> *To the Editor: I would like to know what kind of goddamn govment this is that discriminates between two common carriers and makes a goddam railroad charge everybody equal and lets a goddam man charge any goddam price he wants to for his goddam opera box.*
>
> *W.D. HOWELLS*
>
> *Howells, it is an outrage the way the govment is acting so I sent this complaint to N.Y. Times with your name signed because it would have more weight.*
>
> *MARK*
>
> Mark Twain (1835-1910)

A thorn in the side of the complacent for more than half a century was the Irish-born playwright and critic-at-large, Bernard Shaw. Shaw's views on just about everything set Establishment teeth on edge:

> *He's a man of great common sense and good taste—meaning thereby a man without originality or moral courage.*
> *
> *When a stupid man is doing something he is ashamed of, he always declares that it is his duty.*
> *
> *It is dangerous to be sincere unless you are also stupid.*
> *
> *Do not do unto others as you would that they should do unto you. Their tastes may not be the same.*
>
> Bernard Shaw (1856-1950)

Shaw was an early champion of the plays of Henrik Ibsen; the new, realistic drama was at first universally rejected by the critics:

> *A crazy fanatic ... a crazy cranky being ... not only consistently dirty but deplorably dull.*
> *
> *A wave of human folly.*
> *
> *A gloomy sort of ghoul ... blinking like a stupid old owl.*
>
> Newspaper reviews of Ibsen's
> *Ghosts* and *Hedda Gabler* 1891

Many of Shaw's own plays received an equally nasty welcome:

> *Superabundance of foulness ... wholly immoral and degenerate ... you cannot have a clean pig stye.*
> *
> *Smells to high heaven. It is a dramatized stench.*
>
> Newspaper reviews of Shaw's
> *Mrs. Warren's Profession* 1905

This was a form of rough justice, for Shaw himself did not hesitate to criticize other writers. He was fastidious about the smallest details of how his own work was presented:

> *A more horrible offense against Art than what you*

have put ... on the cover of the Essays, has never been perpetrated even in Newcastle. I reject your handbill with disdain, with rage, with contumelious epithets. ... Of the hellish ugliness of the block of letterpress headed "What the Press says", I cannot trust myself to write, lest I be betrayed into intemperance of language ... Some time ago you mentioned something about changing the cover ... This is to give you formal notice that if you do anything of the sort ... I will have your heart's blood.

Bernard Shaw (1856-1950)
Letter to his publisher

Shaw's self-satisfaction and self-appointed status as a gadfly invoked the wrath of a wide assortment of detractors:

An Irish smut-dealer.

Anthony Comstock (1844-1915)

An idiot child screaming in a hospital.

H.G. Wells (1866-1946)
On Bernard Shaw

George Bernard Shaw, most poisonous of all the poisonous haters of England; despiser, distorter and denier of the plain truths whereby men live; topsyturvey perverter of all human relationships; menace to ordered social thought and ordered social life; irresponsible braggart, blaring self-trumpeter; idol of opaque intellectuals and thwarted females; calculus of contrariwise; flippertygibbet pope of chaos; portent and epitome of this generation's moral and spiritual disorder.

Henry Arthur Jones (1851-1929)

A dessicated bourgeois ... a fossilized chauvinist, a self-satisfied Englishman ... .

Pravda
On Bernard Shaw 1924

But Shaw could outdo them all. In a memorable diatribe, he denounced a bacteriologist, Dr. Edward Bach, who feared the implantation of vicious ape qualities in

80

humans as a result of "monkey-gland" treatments. Shaw's opinion of the human race is never clearer:

> *Has any ape ever torn the glands from a living man to graft them upon another ape for the sake of a brief and unnatural extension of that ape's life? Was Torquemada an ape? Were the Inquisition and the Star Chamber monkey-houses? ... Has it been necessary to found a Society for the Protection of Ape Children, as it has been for the protection of human children? Was the late war a war of apes or of men? Was poison gas a simian or a human invention? How can Dr. Bach mention the word cruelty in the presence of an ape without blushing? ... Man remains what he has always been; the cruelest of all the animals, and the most elaborately and fiendishly sensual.*

Bernard Shaw (1856-1950)

As the twentieth century progressed, the decline of old-fashioned abuse became more apparent. The passionate literary feuds were gone, to be replaced by a more detached, objective — if sometimes equally vicious — form of criticism.

There were exceptions, of course. The inbred world of the universities continued to spawn cutthroat literary infighting. A prime example was A.E. Housman. When he was not writing the barefoot poetry of "A Shropshire

Lad," Housman was a noted classical scholar, whose scalpel could neatly filet those whose work was not up to his standards:

The virtues of his work are quenched and smothered by the multitude and monstrosity of its vices. They say that he was born of human parentage; but if so he must have been suckled by Caucasian tigers. ...

Not only has Jacob no sense for grammar, no sense for coherency, no sense for sense, but being himself possessed by a passion for the clumsy and the hispid he imputed this disgusting taste to all the authors whom he edited.

A.E. Housman (1859-1936)
On Friedrich Jacob

Stoeber's mind, though that is no name to call it by ... turns as unswervingly to the false, the meaningless, the unmetrical, as the needle to the pole.

A.E. Housman (1859-1936)
On Elias Stoeber

One holdover from the old school was the critic Edmund Gosse, who struggled to maintain the proper standards of literature:

My attention has just been called to the current no. of The Sphere, *where Mr. Clement Shorter, in terms of unexampled insolence, speaks of me as "the so-called critic", and attacks me on the score of an article which he has not seen.*

Will you explain to me why I have suddenly received over my head and shoulders this bucket-full of Mr. Clement Shorter's bedroom slops? Can it be that he supposes me to be the author of some attack on him?

If so, pray reassure him. I never attack him, for I never mention him.

Edmund Gosse (1849-1928)
To Thomas Wise

What does pain me exceedingly is that you should

*write so badly. These verses are execrable, and I am
shocked that you seem unable to perceive it.*

Edmund Gosse (1849-1928)
To Robert Nichols

Gosse was particularly outraged by the publication of
James Joyce's monumental *Ulysses*. As far as he could
understand it, he disapproved of it:

*I have difficulty in describing ... the character of
Mr. Joyce's morality. ... he is a literary charlatan
of the extremest order. His principal book,* Ulysses
*... is an anarchical production, infamous in taste,
in style, in everything. ... He is a sort of M. de Sade,
but does not write so well.*

Edmund Gosse (1849-1928)
On James Joyce

So did almost everyone else —

*The work of a queasy undergraduate scratching his
pimples.*

Virginia Woolf (1882-1941)
On James Joyce

*It is written by a man with a diseased mind and soul
so black that he would even obscure the darkness of
hell.*

Senator Reed Smoot
On James Joyce

including, surprisingly, D.H. Lawrence, who found the
work immoral:

*The last part of it is the dirtiest, most indecent, most
obscene thing ever written. Yes it is, Frieda ... it is
filthy.*
*
My God, what a clumsy olla putrida *James Joyce
is! Nothing but old fags and cabbage-stumps of
quotations from the Bible and the rest, stewed in the
juice of deliberate, journalistic dirty-mindedness.*

D.H. Lawrence (1885-1930)
On James Joyce

Lawrence, himself the recipient of many accusations of obscenity, was not made more charitable by criticism. He had a truly nasty tongue, and he scattered his largesse indiscriminately:

> *I loathe you. You revolt me stewing in your consumption. ... The Italians were quite right to have nothing to do with you.*
>
> D.H. Lawrence (1885-1930)
> To Katherine Mansfield

> *Spit on her for me when you see her, she's a liar out and out. As for him, I reserve my language. ... Vermin, the pair of 'em.*
>
> D.H. Lawrence (1885-1930)
> On Katherine Mansfield and J. Middleton Murray

> Never *adapt yourself. Kick Brill in the guts if he tries to come it over you. Kick all America in the guts: they need it. ... Spit on every neurotic, and wipe your feet on his face if he tries to drag you down to him. ... All that "arty" and "literary" crew, I know them, they are smoking, steaming shits.*
>
> D.H. Lawrence (1885-1930)
> To Mabel Dodge Luhan

Occasionally a note of humor crept in, as in his comment on a damning review of his paintings by T.W. Earp:

> *I heard a little chicken chirp:*
> *My name is Thomas, Thomas Earp,*
> *and I can neither paint nor write,*
> *I can only put other people right.*
>
> D.H. Lawrence (1885-1930)

But Lawrence's characteristic attitude was one of rage against all the dolts who would not appreciate him:

> *Curse the blasted, jelly-boned swines, the slimy, the belly-wriggling invertebrates, the miserable sodding rotters, the flaming sods, the snivelling, dribbling, dithering, palsied, pulseless lot that make up England today. They've got white of egg in their veins, and their spunk is that watery it's a marvel they can breed. They can nothing but frog-spawn — the gibberers! God, how I hate them!*
>
> D.H. Lawrence (1885-1930)

This type of vitriol was now the exception. The new writers and critics were in the Oscar Wilde tradition, skewering their victims with witty and sophisticated phrases. The moving spirits were the scintillating group whose headquarters was the Round Table of the Algonquin Hotel in New York, and the zenith of this art form was reached in the drama reviews of the 1930s (although there are earlier examples):

> Hook and Ladder *is the sort of play that gives failures a bad name.*
>
> Walter Kerr (b. 1913)

> *He played the King as though under momentary apprehension that someone else was about to play the ace.*
>
> Eugene Field (1850-1895)
> On actor Creston Clarke's performance as King Lear

> *Tallulah Bankhead barged down the Nile last night as Cleopatra — and sank.*
>
> John Mason Brown (b. 1900)

Very well then: I say Never.
George Jean Nathan (1882-1958)
On *Tonight or Never*

It was one of those plays in which all the actors unfortunately enunciated very clearly.
Robert Benchley (1889-1945)

He has delusions of adequacy.
Walter Kerr (b. 1913)
On an anonymous actor

The scenery was beautiful but the actors got in front of it. The play left a taste of lukewarm parsnip juice.
Alexander Woollcott (1887-1943)

Katherine Hepburn ran the whole gamut of emotions from A to B.
Dorothy Parker (1893-1967)

The brightest star in this firmament was Dorothy Parker—brittle, perceptive, salty, endowed with fast reflexes and an acid wit:

A combination of Little Nell and Lady Macbeth.
Alexander Woollcott (1887-1943)
On Dorothy Parker

Her reviews of books and plays reflect these qualities:

The affair between Margot Asquith and Margot Asquith will live as one of the prettiest love stories in all literature.
On a four-volume autobiography
*
This is not a novel to be tossed aside lightly. It should be thrown with great force.
*
Tonstant Weader fwowed up.
On *The House at Pooh Corner*
In her column "Constant Reader"

Dorothy Parker was also adept at a pointed pun—as when, at a Hallowe'en party, she remarked:

Ducking for apples—change one letter and it's the story of my life.
Dorothy Parker (1893-1967)

The eccentric style of Gertrude Stein provoked a devastating parody-cum-rejection slip from her editor:

I am only one, only one, only one. Only one being, one at the same time. Not two, not three, only one. Only one life to live, only sixty minutes in one hour. Only one pair of eyes. Only one brain. Only one being. Being only one, having only one pair of eyes, having only one time, having only one life, I cannot read your MS three or four times. Not even one time. Only one look, only one look is enough. Hardly one copy would sell here. Hardly one. Hardly one.

A.J. Fifield
To Gertrude Stein

H.L. Mencken was a provocative newspaper columnist whose irreverence inevitably attracted retaliation. Mencken gleefully published a sampler of the abuse hurled at him.

With a pig's eyes that never look up, with a pig's snout that loves muck, with a pig's brain that knows only the sty, and a pig's squeal that cries only when he is hurt, he sometimes opens his pig's mouth, tusked and ugly, and lets out the voice of God, railing at the whitewash that covers the manure about his habitat.

William Allen White (1868-1944)
On H.L. Mencken

Mr. Mencken talks about truth as if she were his mistress, but he handles her like an iceman.

Stuart P. Sherman
On H.L. Mencken

Mencken, with his filthy verbal hemorrhages, is so low down in the moral scale, so damnably dirty, so vile and degenerate, that when his time comes to die it will take a special dispensation from Heaven to get him into the bottommost pit of Hell.

Jackson News
On H.L. Mencken

87

The present literary scene is relatively calm, but there will always be writers who enjoy hurling verbal brickbats for their own sake. And as long as there is a reading public, literary controversy will not die. Witness this recent flurry in the correspondence columns of the *Manchester Guardian*, between an angry middle-aged playwright and a gaggle of poison-pens:

Sir: Having recently seen St. Joan *in London and* Caesar and Cleopatra *in Sydney, it is clearer to me than ever that Shaw is the most fraudulent, inept writer of Victorian melodramas ever to gull a timid critic or fool a dull public.*

He writes like a Pakistani who has learned English when he was twelve years old in order to become a chartered accountant.

John Osborne

*

Sir: What's wrong with Mr. Osborne shows clearly in what he says about Shaw: Mr. Osborne has no wit about him, and thus he never sees anything as complex or funny.

And another thing: Shaw would never have been guilty of such a racial slur as Mr. Osborne offhandedly committed. Shaw was a good and brilliant man. ... Had he created Mr. Osborne, he would have relieved his heavy dullness with something lovable.

(Prof.) Bert G. Hornback

*

Sir: I suggest that Shaw will be remembered with respect when no one looks back in anger — or any other emotion — at the rabid rantings and pompous twaddle of John Osborne.

Michael Crawford
Manchester Guardian 1977

*

Get stewed: books are a load of crap.

Philip Larkin (b. 1922)

UNMITIGATED NOODLES.
KAISER WILHELM II

THE·LAND·GOD
GAVE·TO·CAIN·

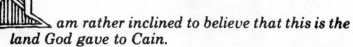 *am rather inclined to believe that this is the land God gave to Cain.*

Jacques Cartier (1491-1557)
On Labrador

Breathes there the man with soul so dead,
Who never to himself hath said
"This is mine own, my native land"?

Sir Walter Scott (1771-1832)

Probably not. And one of the offshoots of strong national pride is the tendency to exalt one's own country by denigrating others. Every country in the world has been derided by the citizens of other lands, pained or outraged that the object of their scorn does not measure up to their own high standards. Tourists and emigrants are particularly prone to contrast the people and customs they meet on their journeys with those wonderful ones they left home to escape.

No nation on earth has suffered more slings and arrows than England. Nearly two thousand years of relationships with other peoples have ensured this. The English have found disfavor with the Romans, the French, the Spanish, the Dutch, the Germans and, more recently, the Americans — and in not a few cases, the feeling has mounted to a passionate hatred.

Poltroons, cowards, skulkers and dastards.

Eustache Deschamps (fourteenth century)

England, the heart of a rabbit in the body of a lion,
The jaws of a serpent, in an abode of popinjays.

Eugene Deschamps (fourteenth century)

The perfidious, haughty, savage, disdainful, stupid,
slothful, inhospitable, inhuman English.

Julius Caesar Scaliger (1540-1609)

Paralytic sycophants, effete betrayers of humanity, carrion-eating servile imitators, arch-cowards and collaborators, gang of women-murderers, degenerate rabble, parasitic traditionalists, play-boy soldiers, conceited dandies.

Approved terms of abuse for East German Communist
speakers when describing Britain 1953

Unmitigated noodles.

Kaiser Wilhelm II of Germany (1859-1941)

The earliest tourists were warned of the dangers of British travel:

You must look out in Britain that you are not cheated by the charioteers.

Marcus Tullius Cicero (106-43 BC)

and subsequent commentators agreed that the English were crooked:

In all the four corners of the earth one of these three names is given to him who steals from his neighbour: brigand, robber or Englishman.

Les Triades de l'Anglais 1572

A pirate spreading misery and ruin over the face of the ocean.

Thomas Jefferson (1743-1826)

The most common epithet through the years has been that of "perfidious Albion":

The English are, in my opinion, perfidious and cunning, plotting the destruction of the lives of foreigners, so that even if they humbly bend the knee, they cannot be trusted.

Leo de Rozmital 1456

I know why the sun never sets on the British Empire: God wouldn't trust an Englishman in the dark.

Duncan Spaeth

The defects of the national character are apparently without number. Englishmen are none too bright —

The English are, I think the most obtuse and barbarous people in the world.

Stendhal (Marie Henri Beyle) (1783-1842)

An Englishman will burn his bed to catch a flea.

Turkish proverb

they are indolent —

... They are naturally lazy, and spend half their time in taking Tobacco.

Samuel de Sorbière (1615-1670)

It is related of an Englishman that he hanged himself to avoid the daily task of dressing and undressing.

Johann Wolfgang von Goethe (1749-1832)

unreliable —

The English have no exalted sentiments. They can all be bought.

Napoleon Bonaparte (1769-1821)

puritanical —

A nation of ants, morose, frigid, and still preserving the same dread of happiness and joy as in the days of John Knox.

Max O'Rell (Paul Blouet) 1883

taciturn —

Silence: a conversation with an Englishman.

Heinrich Heine (1797-1856)

inartistic —

The English are not a sculptural nation.

N. Pevsner 1955

These people have no ear, either for rhythm or music, and their unnatural passion for pianoforte playing and singing is thus all the more repulsive. There is nothing on earth more terrible than English music, except English painting.

Heinrich Heine (1797-1856)

hypocritical —

> *What a pity it is that we have no amusements in England but vice and religion!*
>
> Sidney Smith (1771-1845)

and dull —

> *From every Englishman emanates a kind of gas, the deadly choke-damp of boredom.*
>
> Heinrich Heine (1797-1856)

There were those who maintained that the English were not quite as bad as they seemed:

> *I think that those who accuse the English of being cruel, envious, distrustful, vindictive and libertine, are wrong. It is true that they take pleasure in seeing gladiators fight, in seeing bulls torn to pieces by dogs, seeing cocks fight, and that in the carnivals they use batons against the cocks, but it is not out of cruelty so much as coarseness.*
>
> G.L. LeSage 1715

It was difficult to expect anything better of these God-forsaken people, considering the language they had to speak:

> *To learn English you must begin by thrusting the jaw forward, almost clenching the teeth, and practically immobilizing the lips. In this way the English produce the series of unpleasant little mews of which their language consists.*
>
> José Ortega y Gasset (1883-1955)

> *The devil take these people and their language! They take a dozen monosyllabic words in their jaws, chew them, crunch them and spit them out again, and call that speaking. Fortunately they are by nature fairly silent, and although they gaze at us open-mouthed, they spare us long conversations.*
>
> Heinrich Heine (1797-1856)

But most observers seemed agreed that the unfortunate

qualities of the English could be attributed to two factors: their weather —

> *It is cowardly to commit suicide. The English often kill themselves — it is a malady caused by the humid climate.*
>
> Napoleon Bonaparte (1769-1821)

> *The way to endure summer in England is to have it framed and glazed in a comfortable room.*
>
> Horace Walpole (1717-1797)

> *On a fine day the climate of England is like looking up a chimney; on a foul day, like looking down one.*
>
> **Anonymous**

and their food. English tastes and English cookery have always astonished an unbelieving world:

> *Go back, you dissolute English,*
> *Drink your beer and eat your pickled beef.*
>
> *La Repentance des Anglais et des Espagnols* 1522

*The English, who eat their meat red and bloody,
show the savagery that goes with such food.*

J.O. de la Mettrie (1709-1751)

*There are in England sixty different religious sects
and only one sauce.*

Caracciolo (d. 1641)

More recent travellers have continued to be disenchanted
by the level of English cuisine:

> *The average cooking in the average hotel for the
> average Englishman explains to a large extent the
> English bleakness and taciturnity. Nobody can
> beam and warble while chewing pressed beef
> smeared with diabolical mustard. Nobody can exult
> aloud while ungluing from his teeth a quivering
> tapioca pudding.*

Karel Čapek (1890-1938)

Such fare, of course, produced inevitable results:

> *Belching at table, and in all companies whatsoever,
> is a thing which the English no more scruple than
> they do coughing and sneezing.*

H. Misson de Valbourg 1698

Can there be anything left to criticize? Yes — English
clothing:

> *Englishwomen's shoes look as if they had been
> made by someone who had often heard shoes
> described, but had never seen any.*

Margaret Halsey 1938

cold English houses:

> *An Englishman absolutely believes that he can
> warm a room by building a grate-fire at the end of it.*

Stephen Fiske 1869

and even the very windows:

> *English windows open only half-way, either the top
> half or the bottom half. One may even have the
> pleasure of opening them a little at the top and a*

*little at the bottom, but not at all in the middle. The
sun cannot enter openly, nor the air. The window
keeps its selfish and perfidious character. I hate the
English windows.*

Sarah Bernhardt (1844-1896)

That vast and pulsing metropolis, London, horrified
some onlookers with its contrasts:

London! Dirty little pool of life.

B.M. Malabari (b. 1893)

*London, black as crows and as noisy as ducks,
prudish with all the vices in evidence, everlast-
ingly drunk, in spite of ridiculous laws about
drunkenness, immense, though it is really basically
only a collection of scandal-mongering boroughs,
vying with each other, ugly and dull, without any
monuments except interminable docks.*

Paul Verlaine (1844-1896)

The ultimately unforgivable sin of the English, in the
eyes of others, is their infuriating attitude of calm
superiority to the rest of the world:

*In the eyes of the Englishman the Frenchman is a
dog, the Spaniard a fool, the German a drunkard,
the Italian a bandit. . . . Only the Englishman is the
non plus ultra of perfection, and Nature's master-
piece.*

A. Riem 1798-9

*The ordinary Britisher imagines that God is an
Englishman.*

Bernard Shaw (1856-1950)

*

Scotland and Ireland have been the butt of many jokes —
chiefly, it must be admitted, at the hands of their fellow
islanders, the English.

*I have been trying all my life to like Scotchmen, and
am obligated to desist from the experiment in
despair.*

Charles Lamb (1775-1834)

It requires a surgical operation to get a joke well into a Scotch understanding.

Sidney Smith (1771-1845)

DR. JOHNSON: *Sir, it is a very vile country.*
MR. S——: *Well, Sir, God made it.*
DR. JOHNSON: *Certainly he did, but we must remember that He made it for Scotchmen; and comparisons are odious, Mr. S——, but God made Hell.*

Samuel Johnson (1709-1784)

Much may be made of a Scotchman, if he be caught young.

Samuel Johnson (1709-1784)

Sir, . . . the noblest prospect which a Scotchman ever sees, is the high road that leads him to England!

Samuel Johnson (1709-1784)

There are few more impressive sights in the world than a Scotsman on the make.

James M. Barrie (1860-1937)

He is the fine gentleman whose father toils with a muck-fork. . . . He is the bandy-legged lout from Tullietudlescleugh, who, after a childhood of intimacy with the cesspool and the crablouse, and twelve months at "the college" on moneys wrung from the diet of his family, drops his threadbare kilt and comes south in a slop suit to instruct the English in the arts of civilisation and in the English language.

T.W.H. Crosland (1865-1924)
The Unspeakable Scot

*

The Irish are a fair people; they never speak well of one another.

Samuel Johnson (1709-1784)

A servile race in folly nursed,
Who truckle most when treated worse.

Jonathan Swift (1667-1745)

If one could only teach the English how to talk and

the Irish how to listen, society would be quite civilized.

Oscar Wilde (1854-1900)

Give an Irishman lager for a month, and he's a dead man. An Irishman is lined with copper, and the beer corrodes it. But whiskey polishes the copper and is the saving of him.

Mark Twain (1835-1910)

Put an Irishman on the spit, and you can always get another Irishman to turn him.

Bernard Shaw (1856-1950)

*

Surprisingly enough, very few bad things have been said about the United States. Nothing like the immense body of vituperation against England exists. America came of age as a world power only in the mid-twentieth century — at a period when creative invective was almost dead — and as a result has escaped much of the true nastiness older nations have endured.

This is not to say that everyone has always spoken well of America. A constant flow of overseas visitors has come, seen and been unimpressed with American manners and customs. Their condescension and patronizing attitude infuriated Americans — and not the least when the things they said were true!

Knavery seems to be so much the striking feature of its inhabitants that it may not in the end be an evil that they will become aliens to this country.

George III of England (1738-1820)

I am willing to love all mankind, except an American.

Samuel Johnson (1709-1784)

A nineteenth-century traveler was amazed at the extreme manifestations of American social "delicacy:"

On being ushered into the reception room, conceive my astonishment at beholding a square piano-forte with four limbs. *So that the ladies who visited ...*

might feel in its full force the extreme delicacy of the
mistress of the establishment ... she had dressed
all these four limbs in modest little trousers, with
frills at the bottom of them!

Frederick Marryat (1792-1848)

while another was horrified by the less attractive aspects
of good old American hustle:

There is constant activity going on in one small
portion of the brain; all the rest is stagnant. The
money-making faculty is alone cultivated. They are
incapable of acquiring general knowledge on a
broad or liberal scale. All is confined to trade,
finance, law, and small, local provincial informa-
tion. Art, science, literature, are nearly dead letters
to them.

T.C. Grattan (1792-1864)

English visitors, accustomed to the mouldy dampness of
their own houses, constantly complained about central
heating:

The method of heating many of the best houses is a
terrible grievance to persons not accustomed to it,
and a fatal misfortune to those who are. Casual
visitors are nearly suffocated, and constant occupi-
ers killed. An enormous furnace in the cellar sends
up, day and night, streams of hot air, through
apertures and pipes, to every room in the house. ...
It meets you the moment the street-door is opened to
let you in, and rushes after you when you emerge
again, half-stewed and parboiled, into the whole-
some air. The self-victimized citizens, who have a
preposterous affection for this atmosphere, un-
doubtedly shorten their lives by it. Several elderly
gentlemen of my acquaintance, suddenly cut off,
would assuredly have had a verdict of "died of a
furnace" pronounced on their cases, had a coroner
been called.

T.C. Grattan (1792-1864)

Self-appointed gourmets found the culinary scene a
disaster:

... Every broken-down barber, or disappointed dancing-master, French, German or Italian, sets up as cook with about as much knowledge of cookery as a cow has of cowcumbers. In a word, the science of the table is at the earliest stage of infancy in the United States.

T.C. Grattan (1792-1864)

One apparently universal custom met with revulsion from visitors:

I hardly know any annoyance so deeply repugnant to English feelings, as the incessant remorseless spitting of Americans.

Frances Trollope (1780-1863)

America is one long expectoration.

Oscar Wilde (1854-1900)

You never can conceive what the hawking and spitting is, the whole night through. Last night was the worst. Upon my honour and word I was obliged, this morning, to lay my fur-coat on the deck, and wipe the half-dried flakes of spittle from it with my handkerchief: and the only surprise seemed to be, that I should consider it necessary to do so. When I turned in last night, I put it on a stool beside me, and there it lay, under a cross-fire from five men — three opposite; one above; and one below. I make no complaints and show no disgust.

Charles Dickens (1812-1870)

On the whole, Dickens was not favorably impressed with Americans:

Their demeanor ... is invariably morose, sullen, clownish, and repulsive. I should think there is not, on the face of the earth, a people so entirely destitute of humour, vivacity, or the capacity of enjoyment.

Charles Dickens (1812-1870)

Without doubt the critic who upset the Americans most was Frances Trollope, mother of the famous novelist Anthony Trollope. Returning to England after four years' residence in America in the 1820s, her commentary on American life and manners became a *cause célèbre* in both England and the United States. Travelling on a Mississippi steamer, the fastidious Mrs. Trollope was dismayed by American lack of couth:

The total want of all the usual courtesies of the table, the voracious rapidity with which the viands were seized and devoured; the strange uncouth phrases and pronunciation; the loathsome spitting, from the contamination of which it was absolutely impossible to protect our dresses; the frightful manner of feeding with their knives, till the whole blade seemed to enter into the mouth; and the still more frightful manner of cleaning the teeth afterwards with a pocket-knife, soon forced us to feel that we were not surrounded by the generals, colonels and majors of the old world; and that the dinner-hour was to be anything rather than an hour of enjoyment.

Frances Trollope (1780-1863)

Mrs. Trollope found the natives stingy —

I suppose there is less alms-giving in America than in any other Christian country on the face of the globe. It is not in the temper of the people either to give or to receive.

Frances Trollope (1780-1863)

white-faced —

The ladies have strange ways of adding to their charms. They powder themselves immoderately, face, neck, and arms, with pulverised starch; the effect is indescribably disagreeable by day-light, and not very favourable at any time.

Frances Trollope (1780-1863)

and stooped —

I never saw an American man walk or stand well; ... they are nearly all hollow chested and round shouldered.

Frances Trollope (1780-1863)

101

Above all she was repelled by what she felt was gross commercialism:

> *I heard an Englishman, who had been long resident in America, declare that in following, in meeting, or in overtaking, in the street, on the road, or in the field, at the theatre, the coffee-house, or at home, he had never overheard Americans conversing without the word DOLLAR being pronounced between them. Such unity of purpose ... can ... be found nowhere else, except ... in an ant's nest.*
>
> Frances Trollope (1780-1863)

Mrs. Trollope, you will be glad to hear, loved the scenery!

ANTHONY
TROLLOPE
C.1865

Later travellers were less scathing but still found much to criticize. Mrs. Trollope's son did not have a good time in New York:

> *Speaking of New York as a traveller I have two faults to find with it. In the first place there is nothing to see; and in the second place there is no mode of getting about to see anything.*
>
> Anthony Trollope (1815-1882)

while another budding young writer was patronizing:

> *The American has no language. He has dialect, slang, provincialism, accent, and so forth.*
>
> Rudyard Kipling (1865-1936)

Always there was the recurring complaint about American hot air:

Alas, you are parboiled by a diabolic chevaux-de-frise *of steam pipes which refuse to be turned off, and insist on accompanying your troubled slumbers by an intermittent series of bubbles, squeaks and hisses.*

James F. Muirhead

The author of *Vanity Fair* found no improvement in American table-manners:

The European continent swarms with your people. They are not all as polished as Chesterfield. I wish some of them spoke French a little better. I saw five of them at supper at Basle the other night with their knives down their throats. It was awful.

William Makepeace Thackeray (1811-1863)

By this time the foreign critics had been joined by the home-grown; henceforth it was to be a mixed chorus:

The Americans, like the English, probably make love worse than any other race.

Walt Whitman (1819-1892)

"The American Nation in the Sixth Ward is a fine people," he says. "They love th' eagle," he says, "on the back iv a dollar."

Finley Peter Dunne (1867-1936)
Mr. Dooley

Of course, America had often been discovered before Columbus, but it had always been hushed up.

Oscar Wilde (1854-1900)

America is the only nation in history which miraculously has gone directly from barbarism to degeneration without the usual interval of civilization.

Georges Clemenceau (1841-1929)

It is absurd to say that there are neither ruins nor

103

curiosities in America when they have their mothers and their manners.

Oscar Wilde (1854-1900)

The 100% American is 99% an idiot.

Bernard Shaw (1856-1950)

When you become used to never being alone, you may consider yourself Americanized.

André Maurois (1885-1967)

American women expect to find in their husbands the perfection that English women only hope to find in their butlers.

W. Somerset Maugham (1874-1965)

The trouble with America is that there are far too many wide open spaces surrounded by teeth.

Charles Luckman

Don't get the idea that I'm one of these goddam radicals. Don't get the idea that I'm knocking the American system.

Al Capone (1899-1947)

You are right in your impression that a number of persons are urging me to come to the United States.

But why on earth do you call them my friends?
Bernard Shaw (1856-1950)

The thing that impresses me most about America is the way parents obey their children.
The Duke of Windsor (1894-1972)

No one ever went broke underestimating the taste of the American public.
H.L. Mencken (1880-1956)

Regionalism thrives in the United States, and some states and cities attract criticism as honey does flies. Texas is a favorite target:

If I owned Texas and Hell, I would rent out Texas and live in Hell.
General Philip H. Sheridan (1831-1888)

and so is big, bad New York:

If there ever was an aviary overstocked with jays it is that Yaptown-on-the-Hudson called New York.
O. Henry (1862-1910)

New York — A city of 7,000,000 so decadent that when I leave it I never dare look back lest I turn into

*salt and the conductor throw me over his left
shoulder for good luck.*

Frank Sullivan

Prim, correct Boston has its eccentricities:

*Boston is a moral and intellectual nursery always
busy applying first principles to trifles.*

George Santayana (1863-1952)

while Chicago has occasionally been compared to
another warm spot:

*Here is the difference between Dante, Milton, and
me. They wrote about hell and never saw the place. I
wrote about Chicago after looking the town over for
years and years.*

Carl Sandburg (1878-1967)

The new western mecca is a universal source of fun:

*California is a fine place to live in — if you happen
to be an orange.*

Fred Allen

*His great aim was to escape from civilization, and,
as soon as he had money, he went to Southern
California.*

Anonymous

along with its most notorious community:

*Hollywood is a sewer with service from the Ritz
Carlton.*

Wilson Mizner

*They know only one word of more than one syllable
here, and that is fillum.*

Louis Sherwin
On Hollywood

Perhaps Mark Twain summed up what many observers
still feel about the United States:

*It was wonderful to find America, but it would have
been more wonderful to miss it.*

Mark Twain (1835-1910)

Mme de Pompadour

Canada, a country with a relatively small population and no pretentions to power, has not attracted cataracts of outside criticism; those who noticed her at all tended to dismiss her:

> *You know that these two nations are at war for a few acres of snow, and that they are spending ... more than all Canada is worth.*
>
> Voltaire (1694-1778)

> *It makes little difference; Canada is useful only to provide me with furs.*
>
> Madame de Pompadour (1721-1764)
On the fall of Quebec

> *I fear that I have not got much to say about Canada, not having seen much; what I got by going to Canada was a cold.*
>
> Henry David Thoreau (1817-1862)

> *I don't even know what street Canada is on.*
>
> Al Capone (1899-1947)

while those who probed a little deeper found a depressing stagnation:

Canada is a country without a soul ... live, but not like the States, kicking.

Rupert Brooke (1887-1915)

As false as a diamond from Canada.

Popular French saying, after 1542

Feller Citizens, this country is goin' to the dogs hand over hand.

T.C. Haliburton (1795-1861)
Sam Slick

For many years Canadians accepted their lack of consequence humbly, and rather self-righteously made a virtue of it:

There are too many nasty little self-centred nations in the world already; God forbid that Canada should add one to the number!

W.L. Grant (1872-1935)

They have been wont to define themselves in deprecating terms:

A Canadian is somebody who knows how to make love in a canoe.

Pierre Berton 1973

A Canadian is someone who drinks Brazilian coffee from an English teacup, and munches a French pastry while sitting on his Danish furniture, having just come home from an Italian movie in his German car. He picks up his Japanese pen and writes to his Member of Parliament to complain about the American takeover of the Canadian publishing business.

Campbell Hughes 1973

The Canadian imagination has always been dominated by the climate:

This gloomy region, where the year is divided into one day and one night, lies entirely outside the stream of history.

W.W. Reade 1872

Canada has a climate nine months' winter and three months late in the fall.

American saying (late nineteenth century)

Canada's first novelist did not find the weather an incentive in her work:

I no longer wonder the elegant arts are unknown here; the rigour of the climate suspends the very powers of the understanding: what then must become of those of the imagination? ... Genius will never mount high, where the faculties of the mind are benumbed half the year.

Frances Brooke (1745-1789)

The absence of the elegant arts and the general philistinism of Canadians were bemoaned by foreigners and native-born alike:

The cold narrow minds, the confined ideas, the bygone prejudices of the society are hardly conceivable; books there are none, nor music, and as to pictures! — the Lord deliver us from such! The people do not know what a picture is.

Anna Jameson (1794-1860)

The only poet in Canada was very nice to me in Ottawa. Canada's a bloody place for a sensitive real poet like this to live all his life in.

Rupert Brooke (1887-1915)

Tonight I give lecture to Art Students' League. I want a picture of a horse to show that animal is beautiful because every part made for function, without ornament. In Paris I would show woman, but in Toronto I show a horse.

Anonymous French artist 1931

An early poet struck a note of frustration —

How utterly destitute of all light and charm are the intellectual conditions of our people and the institutions of our public life! How barren! How barbarous!

Archibald Lampman (1861-1899)

109

but a popular comedian has supplied a solution:

> *Support your fellow Canadians. We should buy lousy Canadian novels instead of importing lousy American novels.*
>
> Johnny Wayne 1968

The precarious co-existence between English and **French** in Canada has provided a stimulating national **sport:**

> *That the two tribes of men, French and English, do not assimilate is no new discovery; it is nothing more than Nature herself did when she deliberately created the British Channel.*
>
> Sir Francis Bond Head (1793-1875)

> *English was good enough for Jesus Christ.*
>
> Ralph Melnyk
> On bilingualism

> *All pro athletes are bilingual. They speak English and profanity.*
>
> Gordie Howe 1975

Like the United States, Canada is a country of **regions, and each** province has its own special charms:

I find that Newfoundland is said to be celebrated for its codfish, its dogs, its hogs, its fogs!

Sir William Whiteway (1828-1908)
Former Prime Minister of Newfoundland

The purity of the air of Newfoundland is without doubt due to the fact that the people of the outports never open their windows.

J.G. Millais 1907

A rascally heap of sand, rock and swamp, called Prince Edward Island, in the horrible Gulf of St. Lawrence; that lump of worthlessness ... bears nothing but potatoes ...

William Cobbett (1762-1835)

Good God, what sums the nursing of that ill-throven, hardvisaged and ill-favoured brat, Nova Scotia, has cost to this wittol nation.

Edmund Burke (1729-1797)

Quebec does not have opinions — only sentiments.

Sir Wilfrid Laurier (1841-1919)

Quebec is not a province like the others. She is a little more stupid.

Gérard Filion 1963

Let the Eastern bastards freeze in the dark!

Alberta bumper sticker 1973

British Columbia is a barren, cold, mountain country that is not worth keeping. ... the place has been going from bad to worse. Fifty railroads would not galvanise it into prosperity.

Henry Labouchère (1798-1869)

A number of Canadian cities have endeared themselves to the nation — Halifax:

We have upwards of one hundred licensed houses and perhaps as many more ... without license; so that the business of one half of the town is to sell rum and the other half to drink it.

Anonymous 1760

111

Montreal:

O God! O Montreal!

Samuel Butler (1835-1902)
A Psalm of Montreal

Montreal is the only place where a good French accent isn't a social asset.

Brendan Behan (1923-1964)

Ottawa, the capital:

A sub-arctic lumber village converted by royal mandate into a political cock-pit.

Goldwin Smith (1823-1910)

Kingston:

Indeed, it may be said of Kingston, that one-half appears to be burnt down, and the other half not to be built up.

Charles Dickens (1812-1870)

Winnipeg:

So this is Winnipeg; I can tell it's not Paris.

Bob Edwards (1864-1922)

Medicine Hat:

You people in this district seem to have all Hell for a basement.

Rudyard Kipling (1865-1936)

and of course, Toronto. Hating Toronto is the second national sport:

The situation of the town is very unhealthy, for it stands on a piece of low marshy land, which is better calculated for a frog-pond or beaver meadow than for the residence of human beings.

Edward Talbot (1801-1839)

Houses of ill-fame in Toronto? Certainly not. The whole city is an immense house of ill-fame.

C.S. Clark (1826-1909)

Toronto as a city carries out the idea of Canada as a

112

country. It is a calculated crime both against the aspirations of the soul and the affection of the heart.

Even that scenic wonder, Niagara Falls, has found carping critics:

Niagara Falls is simply a vast unnecessary amount of water going the wrong way and then falling over unnecessary rocks.
Oscar Wilde (1854-1900)

When I first saw the falls I was disappointed in the outline. Every American bride is taken there, and the sight must be one of the earliest, if not the keenest, disappointments of American married life.
Oscar Wilde (1854-1900)

*

Hardly a country on earth has escaped having its tenderest patriotic feelings trampled. The French have been assailed for some well-known national qualities:

France was long a despotism tempered by epigrams.
Thomas Carlyle (1795-1881)

Your nation is divided into two species: the one of idle monkeys who mock at everything; and the other of tigers who tear.
Voltaire (1694-1778)

How can one conceive of a one-party system in a country that has over two hundred varieties of cheeses?
Charles de Gaulle (1890-1970)

while the Germans have attracted solemn observations:

The German mind has a talent for making no mistakes but the very greatest.
Clifton Fadiman (b. 1904)

One thing I will say for the Germans, they are always perfectly willing to give somebody else's land to somebody else.
Will Rogers (1879-1935)

Life is too short to learn German.
Richard Porson (1759-1808)

The Chinese are inscrutable:

There are only two kinds of Chinese — those who give bribes and those who take them.
Russian proverb

the Greeks wily:

Greeks tell the truth, but only once a year.
Russian proverb

After shaking hands with a Greek, count your fingers.
Albanian proverb

and the Russians enigmatic:

Russia — a riddle wrapped in a mystery inside an enigma.
Winston Churchill (1874-1965)

Make ye no truce with Adam-zad — the bear that walks like a man.
Rudyard Kipling (1865-1936)

*

Comparisons are odious, but probably inevitable:

Canada could have enjoyed:
   English government,
     French culture,
       and American know-how.

Instead it ended up with:
   English know-how,
     French government,
       and American culture.
John Robert Colombo 1965

*

The final choice, of course, is between two countries from which no traveler returns:

Heaven for climate; Hell for society.
Mark Twain (1835-1910)

TALKING·OF·THE·BADNESS
OF·THE·GOVERNMENT·

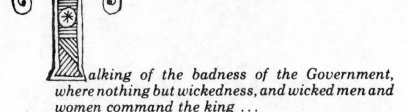

alking of the badness of the Government, where nothing but wickedness, and wicked men and women command the king ...

Samuel Pepys (1633-1703)

Pepys was in good company, for "talking of the badness of the government" is a pastime as old as history. Like the Psalmist and the Bard, the world has always sat in judgment on its rulers.

Put not your trust in princes.

Psalm 146:3

Mad world! Mad kings! mad composition!

William Shakespeare (1564-1616)
King John

Kings is mostly rapscallions.

Mark Twain (1835-1910)

If, as Longfellow asserts,

Lives of great men all remind us
We can make our lives sublime.

they also remind us that great leaders frequently have feet of clay. It may be a degree of comfort to contemporary politicians to realize that few of them have been reviled in such sweeping terms as some of the outstanding figures of history. Men such as George Washington and Thomas Jefferson have become near-deities; but in their own times they were just politicians, fair game for criticism. The man who was to become known as The Father of His Country was reviled by his contemporaries as:

The man who is the source of all the misfortunes of our country.

William Duane (1760-1835)
On George Washington

That dark designing sordid ambitious vain proud arrogant and vindictive knave.

Gen. Charles Lee (1731-1782)
On George Washington

The American press, then as now unimpressed by their chief executive, editorialized sonorously:

If ever a nation was debauched by a man, the American nation has been debauched by Washington. ...If ever a nation was deceived by a man, the American nation has been deceived by Washington.

Benjamin F. Bache (1769-1798)
Aurora

Washington was despaired of —

...and as to you, sir, treacherous in private friendship ... and a hypocrite in public life, the world will be puzzled to decide whether you are an apostate or an imposter, whether you have abandoned good principles, or whether you ever had any?

Tom Paine (1737-1809)
On George Washington

and told to mend his ways —

If you could for a short time ... condescend to that state of humility, in which you might hear the real sentiments of your fellow citizens ... you would save the wreck of character now crumbling to pieces under the tempest of universal irritation not to be resisted.

William Duane (1760-1835)
Aurora

before death brought him the honor which has since been his.

... the immortal leader of the American armies to independence, George Washington, lately deceased.
Aurora 1799

Thomas Jefferson, the sainted author of the Declaration

of Independence, was denounced by one of his fellow founding fathers:

The moral character of Jefferson was repulsive. Continually puling about liberty, equality and the degrading curse of slavery, he brought his own children to the hammer, and made money of his debaucheries.

Alexander Hamilton (1757-1804)

while a future president considered him:

... a slur upon the moral government of the world.

John Quincy Adams (1767-1848)
On Thomas Jefferson

and another political opponent made the judgment that he was:

...a mean-spirited, low-livered fellow ... there could be no question he would sell his country at the first offer made to him cash down.

Anonymous
On Thomas Jefferson

Jefferson's election as President was viewed with apprehension:

Murder, robbery, rape, adultery and incest will be openly taught and practised, the air will be rent with the cries of distress, the soil soaked with blood, and the nation black with crimes. Where is the heart that can contemplate such a scene without shivering with horror?

The New England Courant
On the election of Thomas Jefferson 1800

Extravagant abuse was not the sole province of revolutionary democracies; a whole succession of English monarchs has been roundly cursed, some in detail —

... a pig, an ass, a dunghill, the spawn of an adder, a basilisk, a lying buffoon, a mad fool with c frothy mouth ... a lubberly ass ... a frantic madman ...

Martin Luther (1483-1546)
On Henry VIII

some succinctly —

Cursed Jezebel of England!

John Knox (1505-1572)
On Queen Mary I ("Bloody Mary")

and some in verse!

Here lies our mutton-loving King
Whose word no man relies on.
Who never said a foolish thing,
And never did a wise one.

The Earl of Rochester (1647-1680)
On Charles II

To which Charles is said to have replied, "True, for my words are my own, but my deeds are my ministers'."

In Quebec a century later, Thomas Walker, a merchant disgruntled by the passage of the Quebec Act in 1774, thus defaced the statue of the reigning monarch, George III:

Behold the Pope of Canada and the English Sot.

Even the staid Queen Victoria has not been spared by posterity:

Nowadays, a parlour maid as ignorant as Queen Victoria was when she came to the throne, would be classed as mentally defective.

Bernard Shaw (1856-1950)

The unlovely Hanoverian monarchs seem to have attracted more abuse than even they deserved. Few insults to royalty can match the studied insolence of Beau Brummell's remark to Beau Nash, as the latter entered on the arm of the Prince Regent, later George IV:

Who's your fat friend?

George "Beau" Brummell (1778-1840)

The fashionable Brummell escaped punishment, but the poet Leigh Hunt went to prison for his mild commentary on the Prince Regent:

A corpulent Adonis of fifty.

Leigh Hunt (1784-1859)

and the same vindictive monarch attracted this sentiment:

> *A more contemptible, cowardly, selfish, unfeeling*
> *dog does not exist than this King ... with vices and*
> *weaknesses of the lowest and most contemptible*
> *order.*
>
> Charles Greville (1794-1865)

A traditional form of political invective is verse — often anonymous doggerel. Occasionally a public figure attracts the animosity of a well-known poet, and then the luckless victim may be memorialized forever.

> *George the Third*
> *Ought never to have occurred.*
> *One can only wonder*
> *At so grotesque a blunder.*
>
> E. Clerihew Bentley (1875-1956)

> *I sing the Georges Four,*
> *For Providence could stand no more.*
> *Some say that far the worst*
> *Of all the Four was George the First.*
> *But yet by some 'tis reckoned*
> *That worser still was George the Second.*
> *And what mortal ever heard*
> *Any good of George the Third?*
> *When George the Fourth from earth descended,*
> *Thank God the line of Georges ended.*
>
> Walter Savage Landor (1775-1864)

> *A noble, nasty race he ran*
> *Superbly filthy and fastidious;*
> *He was the world's first gentleman,*
> *And made the appellation hideous.*
>
> W.M. Ptaed
> On George IV

Oliver Cromwell, England's prickly Lord Protector, received his share of abuse, although the spirit of the age did not permit the frivolity of verse. According to his own doctor, who had the benefit of a close view, Cromwell was

A perfect master of all the arts of simulation: who, turning up the whites of his eyes, and seeking the Lord with pious gestures, will weep and pray, and cant most devoutly, till an opportunity offers of dealing his dupe a knock-down blow under the short ribs.

George Bate (1608-1669)

Just before Cromwell's death, some of his erstwhile supporters made haste to ingratiate themselves with the future king by denouncing their leader:

... that grand imposter, that loathsome hypocrite, that detestable traitor, that ... opprobrium of mankind, that landscape of iniquity, that sink of sin, that compendium of baseness, who now calls himself our Protector. Group of English Anabaptists
To the future Charles II 1658

The judgments of posterity have been almost as harsh:

He lived a hypocrite and died a traitor.

John Foster (1770-1843)
On Oliver Cromwell

The Curse of Cromwell on you!

Irish curse

But those who ruled were perfectly capable of returning the same coin, although the habit of command made them more succinct. Queen Elizabeth issued a peremptory threat to a wayward churchman:

Proud Prelate:
You know what you were before I made you what you are now. If you do not immediately comply with my request, I will unfrock you, by God.

Elizabeth I (1533-1603)
To the Bishop of Ely

and Cromwell's dismissal of the Rump Parliament was a model of brevity:

You have stayed in this place too long, and there is no health in you. In the name of God, go!

Oliver Cromwell (1599-1658)

Reader, suppose you were an idiot; and suppose you were a member of Congress; but I repeat myself.

Mark Twain (1835-1910)

The developing democracy of the United States provided a fertile field for political invective. If politicians in every age and country have been the targets of abuse, it must be admitted that they initiated a large percentage of it themselves. The rough and tumble of partisan politics encourages political and personal animosities, many not entirely genuine. It was sometimes useful to pursue them:

There is not a man in the United States so perfectly hated by the people of my district as yourself. You must therefore excuse me. I must abuse you, or I shall never get re-elected.

Anonymous member of Continental Congress
To Josiah Quincy

In the early days of the United States Congress, the House of Representatives was dominated by the scathing tongue of John Randolph of Roanoak, Virginia, whose verbal onslaughts became legendary.

Never was ability so much below mediocrity so well rewarded; no, not even when Caligula's horse was made a consul.

John Randolph (1773-1833)
On Richard Rush

He is like a carving knife whetted on a brickbat.

John Randolph (1773-1833)
On Ben Harden

Randolph was not only venomous but brilliant; witness this memorable and devastating image:

He was a man of splendid abilities but utterly corrupt. Like rotten mackerel by moonlight, he shines and stinks.

John Randolph (1773-1833)
On Edward Livingstone

Randolph was widely reputed to be sexually — though not verbally — impotent, a circumstance that brought forth this attack from Tristam Burges, a representative from Rhode Island:

Sir, divine providence takes care of his own universe. Moral monsters cannot propagate. Impotent of everything but malevolence of purpose, they can no otherwise multiply miseries than by blaspheming all that is pure and prosperous and happy. Could demon propagate demon, the universe might become a pandemonium; but I rejoice that the Father of Lies can never become the Father of Liars. One adversary of God and man is enough for one universe.

Tristam Burges
On John Randolph

Stung, Randolph replied:

You pride yourself upon an animal faculty, in respect to which the slave is your equal and the jackass infinitely your superior.

John Randolph (1773-1833)

During the course of a lengthy speech, Randolph was hectored by a representative from Ohio, Philomen Beecher, who kept popping up to cry "Previous question, Mr. Speaker, previous question!" Irritated, Randolph finally brained the gnat:

Mr. Speaker, in the Netherlands a man of small capacity with bits of wood and leather will, in a few

123

moments, construct a toy that, with the pressure of
the finger and thumb, will cry cuckoo! cuckoo! With
less ingenuity and with inferior materials, the
people of Ohio have made a toy that will, without
much pressure, cry "Previous question, Mr. Speak-
er!"

John Randolph (1773-1833)

Randolph was a hazard in casual conversation as well:

STRANGER: *I have had the pleasure of passing your*
house recently.
RANDOLPH: *I am glad of it. I hope you will always do*
it, Sir.

John Randolph (1773-1833)

HENRY CLAY: *I, sir, do not step aside for a scoundrel.*
RANDOLPH: *On the other hand, I always do.*
The two, meeting on a narrow sidewalk in Washington

Small wonder his colleagues had to seek refuge in the
classics to match him:

His face is ashen; gaunt his whole body,
His breath is green with gall;
His tongue drips poison.
Ovid, quoted by John Quincy Adams (1767-1848)
On John Randolph

Looking back on these old debates, one gets a sense of the
cut and thrust of early American politics, during a period
when the use of words as weapons was a highly developed
art.

This man has no principles, public or private. As a
politician, his sole spring of action is an inordinate
ambition.
Alexander Hamilton (1757-1804)
On Aaron Burr

The bastard brat of a Scotch pedlar.
John Adams (1735-1826)
On Alexander Hamilton

I have no doubt that I was compleatly raskeled out
of my Election. I do not regret that duty to my Self to

my Country compels me to expose such viloney ...
Davy Crockett (1786-1836)

He is, like almost all the eminent men of this country, only half educated. His morals, public and private, are loose.
John Quincy Adams (1767-1848)
On Henry Clay

He is certainly the basest, meanest scoundrel that ever disgraced the image of God — nothing too mean or low for him to condescend to.
Andrew Jackson (1767-1848)
On Henry Clay

He prefers the specious to the solid, and the plausible to the true. ... he is a bad man, an imposter, a creator of wicked schemes.
John C. Calhoun (1782-1850)
On Henry Clay

A rigid, fanatic, ambitious, selfishly partisan and sectional turncoat with too much genius and too little common sense, who will either die a traitor or a madman.
Henry Clay (1777-1852)
On John C. Calhoun

Daniel Webster struck me much like a steam engine in trousers.
Sidney Smith (1771-1845)

... the most meanly and foolishly treacherous man I ever heard of.
James Russell Lowell (1819-1891)
On Daniel Webster

Every drop of blood in that man's veins has eyes that look downward.
Ralph Waldo Emerson (1803-1882)
On Daniel Webster

The word liberty in the mouth of Mr. Webster sounds like the word love in the mouth of a courtesan.
Ralph Waldo Emerson (1803-1882)

The gigantic intellect, the envious temper, the ravenous ambition and the rotten heart of Daniel Webster.

John Quincy Adams (1767-1848)

The verbal vitriol that preceded the Civil War did not end with the onset of physical violence, and leading figures like Abraham Lincoln were subject to torrents of abuse even from those on their own side. That paragon of military inactivity, General George McClellan, who later ran against Lincoln, had an excessively low opinion of his commander-in-chief:

The President is nothing more than a well-meaning baboon. ... I went to the White House directly after tea where I found "the original Gorilla" about as intelligent as ever. What a specimen to be at the head of our affairs now!

General George McClellan (1826-1885)
On Abraham Lincoln

as did the press:

Mr. Lincoln evidently knows nothing of ... the higher elements of human nature. ... His soul seems made of leather, and incapable of any grand or noble emotion. Compared with the mass of men, he is a line of flat prose in a beautiful and spirited lyric. He lowers, he never elevates you. ... When he hits upon a policy, substantially good in itself, he contrives to belittle it, besmear it in some way to render it mean, contemptible and useless. Even wisdom from him seems but folly.

New York Post

Filthy Story-Teller, Despot, Liar, Thief, Braggart, Buffoon, Usurper, Monster, Ignoramus Abe, Old Scoundrel, Perjurer, Robber, Swindler, Tyrant, Field-Butcher, Land-Pirate.

Harper's Weekly
On Lincoln

The contemporary reviews of the Gettysburg Address were universally poor:

... an offensive exhibition of boorishness and vulgarity.

... We did not conceive it possible that even Mr. Lincoln would produce a paper so slipshod, so loose-joined, so puerile, not alone in literary construction, but in its ideas, its sentiments, its grasp. He has outdone himself. He has literally come out of the little end of his own horn. By the side of it, mediocrity is superb.

Chicago Times 1863

But the American style was gradually changing, shaped, no doubt, by the development of the country and the growing domination of men with less formal education. The balloon of pomposity tended now to be pricked, not by the rapier of sophisticated wit, but rather by more homespun pointed humor.

There are many examples of this from Lincoln; almost none of his turning on his tormentors with slashing anger. The man could turn a phrase, though:

He can compress the most words into the smallest ideas better than any man I ever met.

Abraham Lincoln (1809-1865)

His argument is as thin as the homeopathic soup that was made by boiling the shadow of a pigeon that had been starved to death.

Abraham Lincoln (1809-1865)
On Stephen A. Douglas

What kills a skunk is the publicity it gives itself.

Abraham Lincoln (1809-1865)
On slavery

The Lincoln style is best demonstrated in his exchanges with his do-nothing general, George McClellan:

Sending men to that army is like shoveling fleas across a barnyard — not half of them get there.

Abraham Lincoln (1809-1865)

If I gave McClellan all the men he asks for they

could not find room to lie down. They'd have to sleep standing up.

Abraham Lincoln (1809-1865)

Major-General McClellan:
I have just read your despatch about sore-tongued and fatigued horses. Will you pardon me for asking what the horses of your army have done since the battle of Antietam that fatigues anything?

Abraham Lincoln (1809-1865)
Telegram to General George B. McClellan

culminating in this laconic and despairing letter:

My dear McClellan: If you don't want to use the army I should like to borrow it for a while. Yours respectfully,

A. Lincoln

Abraham Lincoln (1809-1865)

Meanwhile, the other side in the Civil War produced its own complaints:

I have been up to see Congress and they do not seem to be able to do anything, except to eat peanuts and chew tobacco, while my army is starving.

Robert E. Lee (1807-1870)

Yes, I know Mr. Davis. He is as ambitious as Lucifer, cold as a snake, and what he touches will not prosper.

Sam Houston (1793-1863)
On Jefferson Davis

Mr. Davis's project did not prosper.

That the general public, as well as the politicians, could use the tools of invective is demonstrated in these unsolicited letters:

My dear and venerable old fellow, beware how you proceed, Sir, beware, or something will come over you as a thief in the night, which may not be so agreeable.

Anonymous
Letter to John Quincy Adams

God damn your god damned old hellfired god
damned soul to hell god damn you and god damn
your god damned family's god damned hellfired god
damned soul to hell and good damnation god damn
them and god damn your god damned friends to
hell.

Mr. Peter Muggins
Letter to Abraham Lincoln

The post Civil War era produced a succession of second-rate politicians whose deficiencies were chronicled in campaign jingles and in the jibes of their enemies:

Blaine, Blaine,
We gave him a pain,
The continental liar
From the State of Maine!

Campaign jingle 1884

During Grover Cleveland's presidential campaign he was forced to admit fathering a child out of wedlock. This indiscretion produced a sprightly opposition jingle:

Ma! Ma!
Where's my Pa?
Gone to the White House
Ha! Ha! Ha!

Campaign jingle 1884

but did not prevent his election:

If there was a wire running to the Throne of Grace,
he'd issue orders to Almighty God, remove Christ
Jesus as a Communist and give some Massachu-
setts Mugwump the job ...

William Cowper Brann (1855-1898)
On Grover Cleveland

Other political aspirants met equally vindictive comments:

Why, if a man were to call my dog McKinley, and
the brute failed to resent to the death the damning
insult, I'd drown it.

William Cowper Brann (1855-1898)
On William E. McKinley

*... a wretched, rattle-pated boy, posing in vapid
vanity and mouthing resounding rottenness.*
New York Tribune
On William Jennings Bryan 1896

The irrepressible Teddy Roosevelt was on both the giving
and receiving end of a good deal of abuse:

McKinley has a chocolate-éclair backbone.
Theodore Roosevelt (1858-1915)
On William E. McKinley

*The bestial nature of the indecent horde of pirates,
second storey men, porch climbers, gunmen and
short card dealers who oppose me is now perfectly
manifest.*
Parody of a Roosevelt campaign speech

*At 3 O'clock
on Saturday afternoon
Theodore ROOSEVELT
WILL WALK
on the
WATERS OF LAKE MICHIGAN*
Spurious flyer distributed at the
Republican National Convention 1912

*His idea of getting hold of the right end of the stick
is to snatch it from the hands of somebody who is
using it effectively, and to hit him over the head
with it.*
Bernard Shaw (1856-1950)
On Theodore Roosevelt

The windy oratory of Warren Harding attracted sardonic
criticism from his fellow politicians:

*His speeches leave the impression of an army of
pompous phrases moving over the landscape in
search of an idea. Sometimes these meandering
words would actually capture a straggling thought
and bear it triumphantly a prisoner in their midst
until it died of servitude and overwork.*
Senator William McAdoo (1863-1941)
On Warren Harding

from acid-penned columnists:

> *He writes the worst English that I have ever encountered. It reminds me of a string of wet sponges; it reminds me of tattered washing on the line; it reminds me of stale bean soup, of college yells, of dogs barking idiotically through endless nights. It is so bad that a sort of grandeur creeps into it. It drags itself out of the dark abysm of pish, and crawls insanely up the topmost pinnacle of posh. It is rumble and bumble. It is flap and doodle. It is balder and dash.*
>
> H.L. Mencken (1880-1956)
> On Warren Harding

and from one of the trendiest poets of the day.

> *the only man woman or child who wrote*
> *a simple declarative sentence with seven*
> *grammatical errors is dead*
>
> e.e. cummings (1894-1962)
> On Warren Harding

Harding's successor followed the advice of an earlier era:

> *Never make people laugh. If you would succeed in life, you must be solemn, solemn as an ass. All great monuments are built over solemn asses.*
>
> Senator Thomas Corwin
> To President James Garfield 1881

> *I think the American public wants a solemn ass as a President. And I think I'll go along with them.*
>
> Calvin Coolidge (1872-1933)

> *He looks as if he had been weaned on a pickle.*
>
> Alice Roosevelt Longworth (b. 1884)
> On Calvin Coolidge

> *How can they tell?*
>
> Dorothy Parker (1893-1968)
> On being informed that Calvin Coolidge was dead

The great days of American political invective were waning. But the thirties produced a number of colorful characters who knew how to twist the knife:

131

I have always found Roosevelt an amusing fellow, but I would not employ him, except for reasons of personal friendship, as a geek in a common carnival.

Murray Kempton
On Franklin Delano Roosevelt

The Vice-Presidency ain't worth a pitcher of warm spit.

Vice-President John Nance Garner (1869-1967)

A labor-baiting, poker-playing, whiskey-drinking evil old man.

John L. Lewis (1880-1969)
On John Nance Garner

I could run on a laundry ticket and beat those bums any time.

Fiorello LaGuardia (1882-1947)
Former mayor of New York

... when I call him an s.o.b. I am not using profanity but am referring to the circumstances of his birth.

Governor Huey Long of Louisiana (1893-1967)
On the Imperial Wizard of the Ku Klux Klan

Huey Long was one of the most quixotic figures of the period. His folksy description of Herbert Hoover as a "hoot owl" and Roosevelt as a "scrootch owl" was illuminating:

A hoot owl bangs into the roost and knocks the hen clean off, and catches her while she's falling. But a scrootch owl slips into the roost and scrootches up to the hen and talks softly to her. And the hen just falls in love with him, and the first thing you know, there ain't no hen.

Huey Long (1893-1967)

Long met his match in Secretary of the Interior Harold L. Ickes, who allowed that the governor was

suffering from halitosis of the intellect. That's presuming Emperor Long has an intellect.

Harold L. Ickes (1874-1952)

Ickes was a deceptively soft-footed individual who could razor an opponent with his dry wit:

The General is suffering from mental saddle sores.
Harold L. Ickes (1874-1952)
On General Hugh S. Johnson

He was celebrated for his description of Wendell Willkie as

a simple barefoot Wall Street lawyer
Harold L. Ickes (1874-1952)
On Wendell Willkie

and for his needling of the brash young Republican presidential candidate, Thomas Dewey. He greeted the announcement of Dewey's candidacy with the comment:

Dewey has thrown his diaper into the ring
Harold L. Ickes (1874-1952)

and confided, about a Dewey speech:

I did not listen because I have a baby of my own.
Harold L. Ickes (1874-1952)
On Thomas E. Dewey

His private opinion of Dewey was more devastating:

He is small and insignificant and he makes too much of an effort, with his forced smile and jovial manner, to impress himself upon people. To me he is a political streetwalker accosting men with "come home with me, dear".
Harold L. Ickes (1874-1952)
On Thomas E. Dewey

*

The postwar era brought vast changes to the American political scene, and the old style of political vituperation is no longer in fashion. Television has removed all traces of preoccupation with language, and the fine-tuning of words is no longer an instinct. More and more the press assumes the role of political scourge, while the politicians, preoccupied with their "image" and carefully ghost-written, mince their words.

I always voted at my party's call,
And I never thought of thinking for myself at all!

W. S. Gilbert (1836-1911)

It was in the British House of Commons that the art of verbal slaughter became most highly developed. The physical, adversary layout of the House, with the ministers of the day compelled to answer for their deeds, created a cockpit atmosphere; and the educational system and the society of England put a high premium on verbal facility. One of the earliest recorded wits of the House was Richard Brinsley Sheridan, the famous playwright of *The Rivals* and *The School for Scandal.* His daily conversation in and out of the House had the same sparkle as his plays:

> *The Right Honourable Gentleman is indebted to his memory for his jests and to his imagination for his facts.*
>
> Richard Brinsley Sheridan (1751-1816)
> On the Earl of Dundas

> SHERIDAN *(leading his victim into a trap): Where, oh where shall we find a more foolish knave or a more knavish fool than this?*
> ONE HONOURABLE GENTLEMAN: *Hear, hear!*
>
> Richard Brinsley Sheridan (1751-1816)

Sheridan was also the consummate master of the fully blown image and the sustained torrent of invective.

> *They send all their troops to drain the products of industry, to seize all the treasures, wealth and*

134

prosperity of the country. Like a vulture with their harpy talons grappled into the vitals of the land, they flap away the lesser kites and they call it protection. It is the protection of the vultures to the lamb.

Richard Brinsley Sheridan (1751-1816)
On the East India Company

His crimes are the only great thing about him, and these are contrasted by the littleness of his motives. He is at once a tyrant, a trickster, a visionary and a deceiver. . . . he reasons in bombast, prevaricates in metaphor, and quibbles in heroics.

Richard Brinsley Sheridan (1751-1816)
On Warren Hastings

The dominant figure of the nineteenth-century House was Benjamin Disraeli. The quintessential outsider, Disraeli won his way to the top by sheer brilliance; his incomparable way with words was a major factor in his success.

Disraeli first rose to prominence by single-handedly destroying the leader of his own Conservative party, Sir Robert Peel. Peel, like many a politician before and since, campaigned against his opponents' policy — in this case, free trade — and once in office, reversed himself and adopted that policy holus-bolus. In a series of scathing speeches, Disraeli flayed Peel and ultimately forced a new election, which the Conservatives lost; Disraeli, however, won his seat and the moral leadership of the party.

The Right Honourable Gentleman caught the Whigs bathing, and walked away with their clothes. He has left them in the full enjoyment of their liberal possession and he is himself a strict conservative of their garments.

Benjamin Disraeli (1804-1881)
On Sir Robert Peel

The Right Honourable Gentleman's smile is like the silver fittings on a coffin.

Benjamin Disraeli (1804-1881)
On Sir Robert Peel

The Right Honourable Gentleman is reminiscent of a poker. The only difference is that a poker gives off occasional signs of warmth.

Benjamin Disraeli (1804-1881)
On Sir Robert Peel

Disraeli's guns were then turned on the Liberals:

If a traveller were informed that such a man was the Leader of the House of Commons, he might begin to comprehend how the Egyptians worshipped an insect.

Benjamin Disraeli (1804-1881)
On Lord John Russell

You owe the Whigs a great gratitude, my Lord, and therefore I think you will betray them. For your Lordship is like a favourite footman on easy terms with his mistress. Your dexterity seems a happy compound of the smartness of an attorney's clerk and the intrigue of a Greek of the lower empire.

Benjamin Disraeli (1804-1881)
To Lord Palmerston

The contrast between Disraeli's sparkling wit and Gladstone's earnest pomposity could not have been more striking.

Mr. Gladstone speaks to me as if I were a public meeting.

Queen Victoria (1819-1901)

He has not a single redeeming defect.

Benjamin Disraeli (1804-1881)
On William Ewart Gladstone

He made his conscience not his guide but his accomplice.

Benjamin Disraeli (1804-1881)
On William Ewart Gladstone

Even Gladstone's supporters sometimes found him intolerable.

I don't object to the Old Man's always having the

ace of trumps up his sleeve, but merely to his belief that God Almighty put it there.

Henry Labouchère (1798-1869)
On William Ewart Gladstone

Asked to distinguish between a misfortune and a calamity, Disraeli quipped:

If Gladstone fell into the Thames, that would be a misfortune, and if anybody pulled him out that, I suppose, would be a calamity.

Benjamin Disraeli (1804-1881)

In the House of Commons Disraeli delivered this perfect parody of Gladstone's own style:

A sophistical rhetorician, enebriated with the exuberance of his own verbocity, and gifted with an egotistical imagination, that can at all times command an interminable and inconsistent series of arguments, malign an opponent and glorify himself.

Benjamin Disraeli (1804-1881)
On William Ewart Gladstone

Disraeli's attacks on Gladstone continued to the end. In his last, uncompleted novel, Disraeli caricatured the young Gladstone:

He was essentially a prig, and among prigs there is a freemasonry which never fails. All the prigs spoke of him as the coming man.

Benjamin Disraeli (1804-1881)
On William Ewart Gladstone

The Irish agitator, Daniel O'Connell, was a particular *bête noire* of Disraeli, who once denounced him as

a systematic liar and a beggarly cheat; a swindler and a poltroon. ... He has committed every crime that does not require courage.

Benjamin Disraeli (1804-1881)
On Daniel O'Connell

Sidney Smith had his own solution for O'Connell:

The only way to deal with such a man as O'Connell

is to hang him up and erect a statue to him under the gallows.

Sidney Smith (1771-1845)

Disraeli's wit was visited on a wide range of targets:

He is a self-made man, and worships his creator.

Benjamin Disraeli (1804-1881)
On John Bright

He was the most conceited person with whom I have ever been brought in contact, although I have read Cicero and known Bulwer Lytton.

Benjamin Disraeli (1804-1881)
On Charles Greville

As I sat opposite the Treasury Bench, the Ministers reminded me of one of those marine landscapes not very unusual on the coasts of South America. You behold a range of exhausted volcanoes, not a flame flickers on a single pallid crest, but the situation is still dangerous. There are occasional earthquakes and ever and anon the dark rumbling of the sea.

Benjamin Disraeli (1804-1881)
On the Liberal ministry

Thomas Carlyle, himself noted for remarkable venom, was at last moved to cry out against Disraeli:

How long will John Bull allow this absurd monkey to dance on his chest?

Thomas Carlyle (1795-1881)
On Benjamin Disraeli

The Chamberlains formed one of the prominent English political families of the late nineteenth and early twentieth centuries. Joseph, the father, was a controversial minister in both Liberal and Conservative administrations; his sons were Austen and Neville — the first famous as an advocate of the League of Nations, the latter infamous as the Man of Munich. Throughout the years, all three members of the family attracted their share of criticism:

To have betrayed two political leaders — to have

wrecked two historic parties— reveals a depth of infamy never previously reached, compared with which the thugs of India are as faithful friends and Judas Iscariot is entitled to a crown of glory.

John Burns (1858-1943)
On Joseph Chamberlain

Mr. Chamberlain loves the working man; he loves to see him work.

Winston Churchill (1874-1965)
On Joseph Chamberlain

He always played the game and he always lost it.

Winston Churchill (1874-1965)
On Austen Chamberlain

He looked at foreign affairs through the wrong end of a municipal drainpipe.

Winston Churchill (1874-1965)
On Neville Chamberlain

He has the lucidity which is the by-product of a fundamentally sterile mind. ... Listening to a speech by Chamberlain is like paying a visit to Woolworth's; everything in its place and nothing above sixpence.

Aneurin Bevan (1897-1960)
On Neville Chamberlain

In the depths of that dusty soul there is nothing but abject surrender.

Winston Churchill (1874-1965)
On Neville Chamberlain

As Disraeli dominated the House in the nineteenth century, so Winston Churchill dominated it with words in the twentieth, although for much of that time his was a political voice in the wilderness.

I remember, when I was a child, being taken to the celebrated Barnum's Circus, which contained an exhibition of freaks and monstrosities; but the exhibit on the programme which I most desired to see was the one described as "The Boneless Wonder." My parents judged that the spectacle

> *would be too revolting and demoralizing for my youthful eyes, and I have waited fifty years to see The Boneless Wonder sitting on the Treasury Bench.*
>
> Winston Churchill (1874-1965)
> On Ramsay MacDonald

> *A curious mixture of geniality and venom.*
>
> Winston Churchill (1874-1965)
> On Herbert Morrison

> *The Happy Warrior of Squandermania.*
>
> Winston Churchill (1874-1965)
> On Lloyd George

> *A sheep in sheep's clothing.*
>
> Winston Churchill (1874-1965)
> On Clement Attlee

> *A modest little man with much to be modest about.*
>
> Winston Churchill (1874-1965)
> On Clement Attlee

The unassuming Attlee occasionally responded in kind:

> *Fifty percent of Winston is genius, fifty percent bloody fool. He will behave like a child.*
>
> Clement Attlee (1883-1967)
> On Winston Churchill

The spare, ascetic figure of Sir Stafford Cripps was a favorite target for Churchill and others.

> *There but for the grace of God goes God.*
>
> Winston Churchill (1874-1965)
> On Stafford Cripps

> *He delivers his speech with an expression of injured guilt.*
>
> Winston Churchill (1874-1965)
> On Stafford Cripps

> *Sir Stafford has a brilliant mind — until it is made up.*
>
> Lady Violet Bonham Carter (1887-1969)
> On Stafford Cripps

The election to power of the Labour Party after the Second

World War established new battle lines in the British House of Commons.

> *They are not fit to manage a whelk-stall.*
>
> Winston Churchill (1874-1965)
> On the British Labour Party

> *The Tories always hold the view that the State is an apparatus for the protection of the swag of the property owners. ... Christ drove the money-changers out of the temple, but you inscribe their title deed on the altar cloth.*
>
> Aneurin Bevan (1887-1960)

> *Here is a pretty prospect — an endless vista of free false teeth with nothing to bite.*
>
> Robert Boothby (b. 1900)
> On the National Health Service and continued austerity

Churchill's main challenger in the House during and after the Second World War was the peppery Welsh socialist, Aneurin (Nye) Bevan.

> *I welcome this opportunity of pricking the bloated bladder of lies with the poniard of truth.*
>
> Aneurin Bevan (1897-1960)
> On Winston Churchill

> *He will be as great a curse to this country in peace, as he was a squalid nuisance in time of war.*
>
> Winston Churchill (1874-1965)
> On Aneurin Bevan

> *He never spares himself in conversation. He gives himself so generously that hardly anybody else is permitted to give anything in his presence.*
>
> Aneurin Bevan (1897-1960)
> On Winston Churchill

It was not only on Churchill that Bevan turned his guns. Others on both sides of the House felt the rough edge of his tongue:

> *Please don't be deterred in the fanatic application of your sterile logic.*
>
> Aneurin Bevan (1897-1960)
> To fellow Socialists

141

. . . a dessicated calculating machine.

Aneurin Bevan (1897-1960)
On Hugh Gaitskill

A squalid, backstairs, third-rate Tammany Hall politician.

Aneurin Bevan (1897-1960)
On Herbert Morrison

The juvenile lead.

Aneurin Bevan (1897-1960)
On Anthony Eden

Why should I question the monkey when I can question the organ grinder?

Aneurin Bevan (1897-1960)
Preferring to question the Prime Minister, Churchill,
rather than the Foreign Secretary, Eden

To a fellow M.P. who complained of an unending round of fraternal society luncheons and dinners, Bevan snapped:

You're not an M.P., you're a gastronomic pimp!

Aneurin Bevan (1897-1960)

Nye Bevan, however, was usually seen by his contemporaries as a gadfly, a noisy nuisance, rather than as a major figure.

He enjoys prophesying the imminent fall of the capitalist system and is prepared to play a part, any part, in its burial — except that of a mute.

Harold Macmillan (b. 1894)
On Aneurin Bevan

Although the rivalry of the Harolds, Macmillan and Wilson, did not compare in verbal fireworks with the Churchill-Bevan or Disraeli-Gladstone bouts, it did have its moments:

He has inherited the streak of charlatanry in Disraeli without his vision, and the self-righteousness of Gladstone without his dedication to principle.

Harold Wilson (b. 1916)
On Harold Macmillan

*If Harold Wilson ever went to school without any
boots, it was merely because he was too big for them.*

Harold Macmillan (b. 1894)
On Harold Wilson

*

As in the United States, recent decades have seen a
decline in the level of British political vitriol. But this
level is still higher than that across the Atlantic, and
there are occasional flashes of lightning.

... an overripe banana, yellow outside, squishy in.

Reginald Paget
On Anthony Eden

*Greater love hath no man than this, that he lay
down his friends for his life.*

Jeremy Thorpe (b. 1929)
On a savage Macmillan cabinet shuffle

*He is forever poised between a cliché and an
indiscretion.*

Harold Macmillan (b. 1894)

*

The notorious Profumo scandal provided the impetus for
a verbal sally in the old style. An attack on Profumo by
the rotund Lord Hailsham, a friend of the miscreant,
provoked this searing commentary:

*From Lord Hailsham we have had a virtuoso
performance in the art of kicking a friend in the
guts. When self-indulgence has reduced a man to
the shape of Lord Hailsham, sexual continence
involves no more than a sense of the ridiculous.*

Reginald Paget

*

*What have you done? cried Christine,
You've wrecked the whole party machine.
To lie in the nude may be rude,
But to lie in the House is obscene.*

Anonymous doggerel
Widely quoted during the Profumo affair

143

What a country! Here all the knaves grow rich and the honest men are ruined.

Louis Joseph, Marquis de Montcalm (1712-1759)

Montcalm's early assessment set the tone for future political discussion in Canada. Although the struggles of settling a vast unpopulated territory might sometimes mute the cries of battle, there was never any question that Canadians would view their politicians and those who governed them with the same sour distaste as their British and American cousins.

One of the earliest Canadian political conflicts revolved around the fight to loosen British colonial rule and throw off the control of the ultraconservative Chateau Clique in Lower Canada and the Family Compact in Upper Canada. The views of these worthies were best represented by the doughty Archdeacon John Strachan:

Nobody would ask for the vote by ballot but from gross ignorance; it is the most corrupt way of using the franchise.

The Rev. John Strachan (1778-1867)

Whenever an advocate of reform managed to get elected to the Assembly, Strachan demanded his expulsion:

The law! the law! Never mind the law! toorn him oot, toorn him oot!

The Rev. John Strachan (1778-1867)
Urging the dismissal of Barnabas Bidwell

One Colonial governor, Sir Peregrine Maitland, advised his successor that

> *men who were notoriously disloyal, and whose characters are really detestable are now degrading the legislature of the country by their presence.*
>
> Sir Peregrine Maitland (1777-1854)

The firebrand of the Reformers in Upper Canada was a bantam fighting-cock, William Lyon Mackenzie.

> *He is a little red-haired man about five feet nothing and extremely like a baboon, but he is the O'Connell of Canada.*
>
> John Langton (1808-1894)
> On William Lyon Mackenzie

> *... a singularly wild-looking little man with red hair, waspish and fractious in manner, one of that kind of people who would not sit down content under the government of an angel. ... he seems intent only on picking holes in other men's coats.*
>
> The Hon. Amelia Murray
> On William Lyon Mackenzie

> *... a broken-down pedlar and a notorious disturber of the public mind.*
>
> Sir Francis Bond Head (1793-1875)
> On William Lyon Mackenzie

Extreme in their views, bombastic and stubborn, the fiery Mackenzie and the incredibly inept Governor Francis Bond Head had also in common their diminutive size:

> *Afraid to look me in the face, he sat, with his feet not reaching the ground, and with his countenance averted from me, at an angle of about 70 degrees; while, with the eccentricity, the volubility, and indeed the appearance of a madman, the tiny creature raved in all directions about grievances here, and grievances there.*
>
> Sir Francis Bond Head (1793-1875)
> On William Lyon Mackenzie

> *Although too small to fill the chair, his shoulders*

and the poise of his head did much to counterbal-
ance the lack of nether proportions. His feet, though
unable to touch the floor, were not allowed to dangle
but were thrust out stiffly in front.

Robina Lizars
On Sir Francis Bond Head

No love was lost between the two:

He is, without exception, the most notorious liar in
all our country. He lies out of every pore in his skin.
Whether he is sleeping or waking, on foot or on
horseback, talking with his neighbours or writing
for a newspaper, a multitudinous swarm of lies,
visible, palpable, and tangible, are buzzing and
settling about him like flies around a horse in
August.

Sir Francis Bond Head (1793-1875)
On William Lyon Mackenzie

In the *Colonial Advocate,* Mackenzie heaped burning
coals on the heads of the Family Compact, collectively
and individually:

I had long seen the country in the hands of a few
shrewd, crafty, covetous men under whose manage-
ment one of the most lovely and desirable sections
of America remained a comparative desert.

William Lyon Mackenzie (1795-1861)
On the Family Compact

... a demon ... a hypocrite ... the Governor's
jackal.

William Lyon Mackenzie (1795-1861)
On the Rev. John Strachan

His Majesty's butcher and baker.

William Lyon Mackenzie (1795-1861)
On John Beverley Robinson and John Strachan

Their mothers came to America to try their luck and
were purchased by their sires with tobacco accord-
ing to the quality of the article.

William Lyon Mackenzie (1795-1861)
On the Robinson family

Mackenzie characterized Sir Peregrine Maitland as

one of the lilies of the field; he toils not, neither does he spin.

and delighted in mocking the governor's ceremonial removal from his summer to his winter residence:

the migration from the blue bed to the brown.

Small wonder that his victims snarled in return:

Another reptile of the Gourlay breed has sprung up among us. What vermin!

John Beverley Robinson (1795-1863)
On William Lyon Mackenzie

Mackenzie castigated those who held power, and in an extravagant mixture of irony and vitriol urged his readers to action:

The most extraordinary collection of sturdy beggars, parsons, priests, pensioners, army people, navy people, place-men, bank directors, and stock and land jobbers ever established to act as a paltry screen to a rotten government.

William Lyon Mackenzie (1795-1861)
On the Legislative Council

Tories! Pensioners! Placemen! Profligates! Orangemen! Churchmen! Brokers! Gamblers! Parasites! allow me to congratulate you. Your feet are at last on the people's necks.

William Lyon Mackenzie (1795-1861)

The mounting controversy came to a head in the comic-opera Rebellion of 1837, which its opponents chose to regard as

... the enterprise of a few vain, vicious, feather-brained men; it had neither spirit nor substance, deriving what poor strength it had from enemies of England ... in America.

Sir John W. Fortescue (1859-1933)

Mackenzie became a temporary outlaw, and his name

was henceforth a controversial one for Canadian reformers. The alarmed British government sent Lord Durham to investigate the situation, unwittingly founding a new industry and inaugurating a classic Canadian method for postponing an issue — the Royal Commission of Inquiry. Durham was unimpressed with what he found:

> *Not government merely, but society itself seems to be almost dissolved; the vessel of the State is not in great danger only, as I had been previously led to suppose, but looks like a complete wreck.*
>
> Lord Durham (1792-1840)

Durham produced a report which earned him the nickname "Radical Jack" and, like every Royal Commission report since, was both hailed and condemned:

> *It is a farrago of false statements and false principles ... the most fatal legacy that could have been bequeathed to our American colonies.*
>
> *Quarterly Review* 1839

> *Lord Durham's plan is English, and directly tends to raise a nation of equal and prosperous freemen; the plan of his opponents is Russian, and directly tends to produce a few arrogant, insufferable nobles, and a multitude of wretched, insulted slaves.*
>
> *Upper Canada Herald*, Kingston 1839

Durham's report was accepted and the Canadian colonies lurched toward self-government and ultimate unity. A driving force in the move toward federation, and the dominant Canadian politician of the second half of the nineteenth century, was John A. Macdonald, a Kingston lawyer whose uncanny resemblance to Disraeli went more than skin deep. His ability to lead, prod, cajole, compromise and scheme was largely responsible for the Act of Confederation in 1867; he was Canada's first Prime Minister, and despite scandals and disenchantments he was out of office for only brief periods until his death in

1891. His political demise was often predicted — always prematurely:

Sir John A. Macdonald is about to retire to private life, a thoroughly used-up character.

Toronto *Globe* 1858

Like all successful Canadian political leaders, Macdonald was adroit at delaying issues until they somehow solved themselves or quietly went away. His habits of procrastination earned him a sobriquet that dogged him the rest of his life:

"Old Tomorrow" would be just the name for Sir John.

Col. A.G. Irvine (1837-1916)

His political wiliness led to mixed feelings in more than one opposition M.P.—

Ah, John A., John A., how I love you! How I wish I could trust you!

Anonymous Liberal M.P. 1863

Some of the judgments on him were ambiguous, to say the least:

Had he been a much worse man he would have done Canada much less harm.

Sir Richard Cartwright (1835-1912)

But most observers were more inclined to marvel at his resilience:

Well, John A. beats the devil!

Luther Holton (1817-1880)
On Macdonald's reelection following the Pacific Scandal

Macdonald was frequently exasperated by political opponents. An early example was Sir Oliver Mowat, later Liberal premier of Ontario.

You damned pup. I'll slap your chops for you!

Sir John A. Macdonald (1815-1891)
To Oliver Mowat in Ontario House of Assembly

One of Macdonald's chief opponents in the Confederation negotiations was

> *That pestilent fellow, Howe.*
>
> Sir John A. Macdonald (1815-1891)
> On Joseph Howe

Joseph Howe was a Nova Scotia publisher and leader of a valiant fight for freedom of the press, who seldom minced his words. He was at first an enthusiastic supporter of Confederation:

> *Let the dog return to his vomit rather than Canada to division.*
>
> Joseph Howe (1804-1873)
> To Confederation conference

but whether out of principle, or for other motives,

> *I will not play second fiddle to that damned Tupper.*
>
> Joseph Howe (1804-1873)
> Declining to attend Charlottetown and Quebec Conferences

Howe boycotted the negotiations and became bitterly opposed to the scheme. The pro-Confederation forces were scornful of the doubters:

> *Prince Edward Island will have to come in, for if she does not we will have to tow her into the St. Lawrence.*
>
> Thomas D'Arcy McGee (1825-1868)

Howe weighed in on the other side, dubbing the new plan 'The Botheration Scheme".

> *Messrs. Tupper, Archibold and McCully when the deed is done, may escape to Canada and stifle, as Arnold did, the reproofs of conscience amidst the excitements of a wider sphere and of more lucrative employment. But what is to become of the poor dupes who have been their accomplices in this dark transaction? Nineteen-twentieths of them will live and die at home, and all their lives must behold the averted faces of their indignant countrymen; and creep at last to dishonoured graves in the bosom of*

the province they have betrayed, to poison the worms that consume them beneath the soil to which they were untrue.

Joseph Howe (1804-1873)
"The Botheration Papers"

When, ignoring Howe, the Legislature voted to enter Confederation, Nova Scotia became entitled to a grant of 80¢ per capita as part of the bargain.

We are sold for the price of a sheepskin.

Joseph Howe (1804-1873)

LITTLE BOY: Father, what country do we live in?
FATHER: My dear son, you have no country, for Mr. Tilley has sold us all to the Canadians for eighty cents a head.

Andrew R. Wetmore (1820-1892)
Imaginary dialogue with his son

John A. Macdonald led the Conservatives for nearly forty years; during that time he faced a succession of leaders of the Clear Grits, or Liberals, as the reform party came to be known. Preeminent among these was George Brown, editor of the *Globe,* an irascible, Jovian figure who played Gladstone to Macdonald's Disraeli:

After some five minutes' conversation in the Globe *office with a hungry-looking bald-headed individual in his shirt sleeves, and nails in mourning, I desired to see the Honourable Brown himself. Much to my surprise I found that he stood before me.*

Horton Rhys 1861

The great reason why I have been able to beat Brown is that I have been able to look a little ahead, while he could on no occasion forego the temptation of a temporary triumph.

Sir John A. Macdonald (1815-1891)
On George Brown

Sir John was able to turn his well-known penchant for the bottle into a weapon against the unbending Brown:

I know enough of the feeling of this meeting to know

151

that you would rather have John A. drunk than
George Brown sober.

Sir John A. Macdonald (1815-1891)
Election speech

A later Prime Minister, for fifteen years, was the **elegant,**
sophisticated Wilfrid Laurier.

That damn dancing-master who had bitched the
whole show.

Dr. S. Jameson (1853-1917)
To Rudyard Kipling, on Sir Wilfrid Laurier

A man who had affinities with Machiavelli as well
as with Sir Galahad.

John W. Dafoe (1866-1944)
On Sir Wilfrid Laurier

I would rather do business with a cad who knows
his own mind.

Joseph Chamberlain (1836-1914)
On Sir Wilfrid Laurier

Laurier did not have an excessively exalted view of his
fellow countrymen:

The great mass of the electors are ignorant, and a
great majority of them never read, and remain as
much in the dark as to what is going on in this
country as if they were residing in Europe.

Sir Wilfrid Laurier (1841-1919)
To Edward Blake

Had I been born on the banks of the Saskatchewan,
I would myself have shouldered a musket to fight
against the neglect of governments and the shame-
less greed of speculators.

Sir Wilfrid Laurier (1841-1919)
On the hanging of Louis Riel

Laurier fell out with his party over the conscription issue
during the First World War, and all but a handful of
Liberals abandoned him. When he died four years later,
the unseemly scramble of his erstwhile followers to do
him honor prompted one sardonic onlooker to comment:

Do you think we can trust the bastards with the old man's body?

Charles Murphy (1863-1935)

Nineteenth-century Canadian politics threw up a number of strong personalities, many of them connected with the building of the Canadian Pacific Railway. Donald Smith, later Lord Strathcona, incurred the displeasure of Macdonald:

I could lick that man Smith quicker than hell could frizzle a feather.

Sir John A. Macdonald (1815-1891)
On Donald Smith

It was an age when neither politicians nor press hesitated to call a spade a spade:

He was so flattered and fondled by great men in high offices, that he looked as bewildered with unexpected honours as an interesting young widow giving herself away in matrimony for the fourth time.

On Amos Wright, M.P.P.

How many Canadian M.P.P.s could obtain third-class certificates from the most lenient of our educational examination boards?

R.J. Macgeorge (1811-1884)
Streetsville Weekly Review

The Fisherman who would sell Bait to a Frenchman would steal the pennies off his dead mother's eyes.

Newfoundland political placard
During fishing dispute with France 1886

He has but one principle, that of self-interest. He has only one desire, the desire to insult. He belongs to the school of lying, hypocrisy and cowardice.

E.E. Cinq-Mars
On Sir George Foster 1906

See the faces of the Grits,
    Grizzly Grits,

What a woe-begone expression at
  present o'er them flits.

But the people — they who vote —
  of their twaddle take no note,
For they know the dismal, dreary,
  direful dole
Of the Grits
Of the moribund, morose and melancholy
  Grits, Grits, Grits, Grits,
The greedy, grubby garrulous old Grits.

The People's Almanac 1891

The mud-bespattered politicians of the trade, the
party men and party managers, give us in place of
patriotic statecraft the sordid traffic of a tolerated
jobbery. For bread, a stone. Harsh is the cackle of
the little turkey-cocks of Ottawa, fighting the while
as they feather their mean nest of sticks and mud,
high on their river bluff.

Stephen Leacock (1869-1944)

Canadian political discussion in the middle years of the
twentieth century was conducted in much less acid terms,
partly due to the long prime ministerial tenure of William
Lyon Mackenzie King. Grandson of the old Reformer,
King was the antithesis of his ancestor — cautious,
shrewd, equivocal and the ultimate compromiser. He
enveloped his listeners in a fog of words, through which
his political intentions were barely discernible. Curious-
ly, this outwardly dull man brought out the poet in his
critics, at least one of whom pounced on the personal
eccentricities revealed only after his death.

He skilfully avoided what was wrong
Without saying what was right,
And never let his on the one hand
Know what his on the other hand was doing.

Frank Scott 1957
On W.L. Mackenzie King

William Lyon Mackenzie King
Sat in the middle and played with string;

And he loved his mother like anything —
William Lyon Mackenzie King.

Dennis Lee 1974

Despite its rather bland exterior, politics in Canada **has remained** lively enough in this century; the advent of two **new** political parties, the early activities for women's **rights,** and a number of flamboyant politicians have **ensured** that.

The way to get things out of a government is to back them to the wall, put your hands to their throats, and you will get all they have.

Agnes McPhail (1890-1954)
First woman elected to the Canadian Parliament

I am opposed by all the short-haired women and the long-haired men in the Province.

Sir Rodmond Roblin (1853-1937)

I just hold my nose and mark the ballot.

Frank Underhill
Asked how he could vote Liberal 1967

Those people in Ottawa couldn't run a peanut stand.

W.A.C. Bennett
Former premier of British Columbia 1967

I don't mind someone stealing my pyjamas, but he should wear all of them if he doesn't want to appear indecent.

T.C. Douglas
Former premier of Saskatchewan,
On Liberal appropriation of CCF (NDP) policies 1971

For socialists, going to bed with the Liberals is like having oral sex with a shark.

Larry Zolf 1975

The left in Canada is more gauche *than* sinister.

John Harney 1970

Social Credit once had a war on poverty. Phil Gaglardi started to throw rocks at beggars.

Graham Lead
Former B.C. Minister of Highways 1975

Corporate Welfare Bums!

NDP campaign slogan 1972

No shirt is too young to be stuffed.

Larry Zolf
On Conservative leader Joe Clark 1977

Former Prime Minister John Diefenbaker's zest for parliamentary debate is legendary, and he was always at his best when criticizing. Both the despised Grits and members of his own party, who later deposed him, have felt his verbal lashes:

The Liberals are the flying saucers of politics. No one can make head nor tail of them and they never are seen twice in the same place.

*

When I think of some of the statements made here I begin to think that we are living in a new age of palaeontology — political palaeontology — the invertebrate age, which is government without a backbone.

*

If I were a Roman Catholic, the first thing I would do every morning would be to get down on my knees and ask my God for absolution for ever having appointed McCutcheon to the Senate.

On Wallace McCutcheon, a fellow Conservative

*

... that adjectival authority, pusillanimous and uncertain as he pictures the darkness spreading over Canada.

On Lester B. Pearson

*

Jean Lesage is the only person I know who can strut sitting down.

On the former Premier of Quebec

*

Flora MacDonald is the finest woman to have walked the streets of Kingston since Confederation.

On a rival Conservative

John G. Diefenbaker (b. 1895)

*

I couldn't have called him an s.o.b. — I didn't know he was one — at the time.

John F. Kennedy (1917-1963)
On John G. Diefenbaker

For ten years the Canadian public has carried on a love-hate relationship with the enigmatic Pierre Trudeau.

> *The Hon. Member disagrees. I can hear him shaking his head.*
>
> Pierre Elliott Trudeau (b. 1919)

> *When they get ten steps away from the House of Commons, they are nobodies.*
>
> Pierre Elliott Trudeau (b. 1919)
> On opposition M.P.s

> *In Pierre Elliott Trudeau Canada has at last produced a political leader worthy of assassination.*
>
> Irving Layton (b. 1912)

On one famous occasion, the Prime Minister was accused of "mouthing" the ultimate obscenity in the House. Inspiration striking, Trudeau insisted that the actual phrase was

> *Fuddle-duddle!*
>
> Pierre Elliott Trudeau (b. 1919)

and a disbelieving but amused nation took up the new expression with enthusiasm.

*

Canadians continue to be preoccupied with the century-old concern of political independence:

> *Ours is a sovereign nation*
> *Bows to no foreign will*
> *But whenever they cough in Washington*
> *They spit on Parliament Hill.*
>
> Joe Wallace 1964

*

The last word on the Canadian Parliament was found in the pocket of a critic whose bomb, intended for the Commons chamber, exploded prematurely:

> *Mr. Speaker, Gentlemen, I might as well give you a blast to wake you up. . . . The only bills you pass are the ones that line your pockets, while the rest of the country has to eat spaghetti and meat balls.*
>
> Paul Joseph Chartier 1966

157

The Temper of Democracy

The essence of democratic politics is the right to participate, and the citizen can take a vigorous role in criticizing as well as choosing his rulers. The elected politician has to hone his wit on the often arduous campaign trail. In the sometimes rough, sometimes humorous interchange with hostile voters, a quick mind is a precious asset:

> CONSTITUENT: *Vote for you? I'd as soon vote for the devil!*
> JOHN WILKES: *And if your friend is not standing?*
>
> *
> HECKLER: *Speak up, I can't hear you.*
> DISRAELI: *Truth travels slowly, but it will reach even you in time.*
>
> *
> VOICE IN CROWD: *Give 'em hell, John!*
> JOHN DIEFENBAKER: *I never give them Hell. I just tell the truth and it sounds like hell to the Grits.*
>
> *
> HECKLER: *Don't you wish you were a man?*
> AGNES McPHAIL: *Yes. Don't you?*
>
> *
> HECKLER: *Go ahead, Al. Tell 'em all you know. It won't take you long.*
> AL SMITH: *If I tell 'em all we both know it won't take me any longer.*

But sometimes even an experienced political orator can be outmatched by that most inventive user of invective, the ordinary citizen:

158

EARL WARREN: *I'm pleased to see such a dense crowd here tonight.*

HECKLER: *Don't be too pleased, Governor, we ain't all dense.*

*

MITCHELL HEPBURN: *(at a farm meeting, speaking from a manure spreader) This is the first time in my life that I have spoken from a Tory platform.*

HECKLER: *Throw her in high gear, Mitch, she's never had a bigger load on.*

*

HECKLER: *I'm a Democrat!*

THEODORE ROOSEVELT: *May I ask the gentleman why he is a Democrat?*

HECKLER: *My grandfather was a Democrat; my father was a Democrat; and I am a Democrat.*

THEODORE ROOSEVELT: *My friend, suppose your grandfather had been a jackass and your father was a jackass, what would you be?*

HECKLER: *(instantly) A Republican!*

*

Despite changing styles and intermittent attempts to suppress it, the democratic right to criticize remains intact. Nor do opinions change. Compare these descriptions of two Democratic presidential conventions, a century apart:

> *...the meanest kind of bawling and blowing office-holders, office-seekers, pimps, malignants, conspirators, murderers, fancy-men, custom-house clerks, contractors, kept-editors, spaniels well-train'd to carry and fetch, jobbers, infidels, disunionists, terrorists, mail-riflers, slave-catchers, pushers of slavery, creatures of the President, creatures of would-be Presidents, spies, bribers, compromisers, lobbyers, sponges, ruin'd sports, expell'd gamblers, policy-backers, monte-dealers, duellists, carriers of conceal'd weapons, deaf men, pimpled men, scarr'd inside with vile disease, gaudy outside with gold chains made from the people's money and harlot's money twisted together; crawling, serpentine men,*

the lousy combinings and born freedom-sellers of the earth.

Walt Whitman (1819-1892)
On a Democratic National Convention of the 1850s

*

A man of taste, arrived from Mars, would take one look at a convention floor and leave forever, convinced he had seen one of the drearier squats of Hell ... a cigar-smoking, stale-aired, slack-jawed, butt-littered, foul, bleak, hardworking, bureaucratic death gas of language and faces ... lawyers, judges, ward heelers, mafiosos, Southern goons and grandees, grand old ladies, trade unionists and finks; of pompous words and long pauses which lie like a leaden pain over fever.

Norman Mailer
On the 1960 Democratic National Convention

Plus ça change, plus c'est la même chose. What will they be saying in another hundred years?

* * * * * * * * * * * * * *

Democracy is a form of religion. It is the worship of jackals by jackasses.

H.L. Mencken (1880-1956)

Forgive Thine Enemies

Always forgive your enemies — but never forget their names.
Robert F. Kennedy (1925-1968)

ROBERT KENNEDY

The French, of course, have a word for it — *l'esprit de l'escalier*. Staircase wit — the perfect retort that comes on the way downstairs, long after it would have been useful. Most of us are staircase wits, and we admire all the more those ready spirits who are poised with a verbal stiletto — who jab, prod or run through an opponent as we ourselves can never do.

The effective insult takes many forms. It may be oral and spontaneous, a happy thought striking at just the right moment. Or it may be polished and literary, the careful product of long and malicious effort. At its best it combines an aptness to its subject with a flair for words that leaves even the victim applauding. Pure invective — the piling up of real or fancied indignation into a Niagara of abuse — has its place, and so, too, does the pure wisecrack, although this last must contain at least a kernel of truth to have a staying power beyond the moment. Incivilities, far more than kind words, are revealing: they can tell as much about the perpetrator as his victim.

The creator of an inspired remark surely performs a service to mankind. Consider, for instance, the total picture of personality conjured up by this comment on a notoriously rotund and rumpled journalist:

A one-man slum.

Anonymous; on Heywood Broun

or the pinch-faced image of a somewhat less than memorable U.S. president:

A victim of the use of water as a beverage.

Sam Houston (1793-1863) on James K. Polk

or on the nasal impact of a celebrated novelist:

An animated adenoid.

Anonymous; on Ford Madox Ford

162

The creator of that novel beloved by teenagers, *The Catcher in the Rye*, was skewered by a contemporary who has himself been the target of countless insults:

The greatest mind ever to stay in prep school.
> Norman Mailer (b. 1923) on J.D. Salinger

And, of course, media personalities are always an easy mark:

A legend in his own lunchtime.
> Christopher Wordsworth on
> journalist Clifford Makins

He rose without a trace.
> Kitty Muggeridge on TV interviewer David Frost

Self-revelation can take place either consciously or unconsciously:

I'm as pure as driven slush.
> Tallulah Bankhead (1903-1968) on herself

I liked your opera. I think I will set it to music.
> Ludwig van Beethoven (1770-
> 1827) to a fellow composer

Cool sophistication is at the heart of this icy insult:

He has the heart of a cucumber fried in snow.
> Ninon de Lenclos (1620-1705) on
> the marquis de Sévigné

but a less delicate comparison also gets the message across:

A lamentably successful cross between a fox and a hog.
> James G. Blaine (1830-1893) on
> Benjamin F. Butler

The most successful creative incivility draws a complete and damning picture in a few strokes:

He is every other inch a gentleman.
> Noel Coward (1899-1973) on an
> anonymous novelist

He has a face like a wedding cake left out in the rain.
> Anonymous; on W. H. Auden

The King blew his nose twice, and wiped the royal perspiration repeatedly from a face which is probably the largest uncivilized spot in England.
> Oliver Wendell Holmes (1809-1904) on William IV

although a seemingly gentle verbal twist can also be used to telling effect:

There goes Jim Fisk, with his hands in his own pockets for a change.
> Anonymous; on financier James Fisk

Dr. Donne's verses are like the Peace of God, for they pass all understanding.
> James I (1566-1625) on John Donne

A skeptical female demolished a well-known writer's spurious claims to amorous adventure with one deft masterstroke:

Some people kiss and tell. George Moore told but did not kiss.
> Susan Mitchell on George Moore

while an Oxford don, suave and sophisticated, strove for the elegant approach:

*What time he can spare from the adornment of his person he
devotes to the neglect of his duties.*
> Benjamin Jowett (1817-1893) on
> an undergraduate

and a jovial clergyman put down a self-satisfied friend with ego-
pricking finality:

*I am just going to pray for you at St. Paul's, but with no very
lively hope of success.*
> Sydney Smith (1771-1845) to Monckton Milnes

And then there is the cryptic remark, espoused by those who
must, surely, know what they mean:

*A village explainer, excellent if you were a village, but if you
were not, not.*
> Gertrude Stein (1874-1946) on
> Ezra Pound

The fine art of repartee, the use of the pointed put-down, has
always been cherished. One account records the deflation of a
seventeenth-century actress who was playing a male role:

*This agreable Actress in the Part of Sir Harry coming into the
Greenroom said pleasantly,* In my Conscience, I believe half
the Men in the House take me for one of their own Sex.
Another Actress reply'd, It may be so, but in my Conscience!
the other half can convince them to the Contrary.
> William Rufus Chetwood
> (d. 1766) on actress Peg
> Woffington

The quick retort was a favorite sport even in ancient Greece:

DEMOSTHENES: *The Athenians will kill you some day when they are in a rage.*
PHOCION: *And you, when they are in their senses.*

The witty Bernard Shaw was seldom caught with his defenses down. The gaunt playwright was speaking with a portly newspaper tycoon:

LORD NORTHCLIFFE: *The trouble with you, Shaw, is that you look as if there were a famine in the land.*
SHAW: *The trouble with you, Northcliffe, is that you look as if you were the cause of it.*

When Shaw prepared to take an opening-night bow at one of his plays, a voice from the balcony cried "Boo!"

My friend, I quite agree with you. But what are we two against so many?

Bernard Shaw (1856-1950)

Horatio Bottomley was an arch-charlatan who engaged in a number of dubious financial projects and at last received his just reward. A friend visited Horatio in prison, where he found him stitching mailbags:

VISITOR: *Ah, Bottomley — sewing?*
BOTTOMLEY: *No — reaping.*

Horatio Bottomley (1860-1933)

And then there is this account, possibly even true, of royal weariness with mind-numbing conversation:

OFFICIAL: *And how was your flight, Sir?*
DUKE: *Have you ever flown?*

OFFICIAL: *Oh, yes, Sir, many times.*
DUKE: *Well, it was like that.*

H.R.H. the duke of Edinburgh (b. 1921)

The great Dr. Johnson was afflicted by many hangers-on who tried their best to impress him. One young man lamented the fact that he had now "lost all his Greek":

I believe it happened at the same time, Sir, that I lost all my large estate in Yorkshire.

Samuel Johnson (1709-1784)

One famous and benign father took advantage of an opening that many a parent would welcome:

TOM SHERIDAN: *I think, father, that many men who are called great patriots in the House of Commons are really great humbugs. For my own part, when I get into Parliament, I will pledge myself to no party, but write upon my forehead in legible characters, "To Be Let".*
R. B. SHERIDAN: *And under it, Tom, write "Unfurnished".*

Richard Brinsley Sheridan (1751-1816)

Political debate, of course, lends itself to a ready mind:

LORD CHATHAM: *If I cannot speak standing, I will speak sitting; and if I cannot speak sitting I will speak lying.*
LORD NORTH: *Which he will do in whatever position he speaks.*

Lord North (1732-1792)

VOTER: *Mr. Fox, I admire your head, but damn your heart.*
FOX: *Sir, I admire your candour, but damn your manners.*

Charles James Fox (1749-1806)

VOTER: *You little pipsqueak, I could swallow you in one bite.*

DOUGLAS: *And if you did, my friend, you'd have more brains in your belly than you have in your head.*
> Former premier of Saskatchewan
> Tommy Douglas (b. 1904)

The law courts provide another useful venue for practicing the art of repartee. One sharp-minded judge was faced with a hesitant and stammering young advocate:

BARRISTER: *The unfortunate client — er — on whose behalf I appear — my unfortunate client —*
ELLENBOROUGH: *You may go on, sir. So far the court is with you.*
> Lord Ellenborough (1750-1818)

The silver-tongued Joseph Choate was arguing in a Long Island courtroom:

LAWYER: *Gentlemen, I sincerely hope your decision will not be influenced by the Chesterfieldian urbanity of my opponent.*
CHOATE: *Gentlemen, I am sure you will not be influenced, either, by the Westchesterfieldian suburbanity of my opponent.*
> Joseph H. Choate (1832-1917)

The great F. E. Smith, later Lord Birkenhead, was pleading a case before a muddle-headed judge. Seeing His Lordship's confusion, Smith produced a concise and masterly summary of the evidence. It did not help:

JUDGE: *I am sorry, Mr. Smith, but I am none the wiser.*
SMITH: *No, my Lord. But you are better informed.*
> F. E. Smith (1872-1930)

British Prime Minister Disraeli attended a public dinner where the meal, served from a distant kitchen, was stone cold. As he sipped his champagne after dinner, he was heard to murmur:

Thank God! I have at last got something warm.
Benjamin Disraeli (1804-1881)

On his deathbed, Disraeli was told that Queen Victoria wished to visit him:

No, it is better not. She would only ask me to take a message to Albert.
Benjamin Disraeli (1804-1881)

At the height of his fame, the composer Mozart was approached by a youth who wanted advice on composing a symphony:

MOZART: *You are still very young. Why not begin with ballads?*
YOUNG MAN: *But you composed symphonies when you were only ten years old.*
MOZART: *True — but I didn't ask how.*
Wolfgang Amadeus Mozart (1756-1791)

The artist James Whistler was both quick-witted and notoriously vain:

FRIEND: *There are only two great painters; you and Velasquez.*
WHISTLER: *Why drag in Velasquez?*
James McNeill Whistler (1834-1903)

But once in a while, those who try to deliver a witty insult find that it boomerangs. The legendary U.S. Senator Chauncey Depew was a man of enormous girth, as was President William Taft. It fell to Depew, glancing at Taft's waistline, to make an amusing dinner introduction:

DEPEW: *I hope, if it is a girl, Mr. Taft will name it for his charming wife.*
TAFT: *If it is a girl, I shall, of course name it for my lovely*

helpmate of many years. And if it is a boy, I shall claim the father's prerogative and name it Junior. But if, as I suspect, it is only a bag of wind, I shall name it Chauncey Depew.
                                  William Howard Taft (1856-1930)

Depew rather fancied himself as a phrase-maker, and once again received his comeuppance:

Mr. Depew says that if you open my mouth and drop in a dinner, up will come a speech. But I warn you that if you open your mouths and drop in one of Mr. Depew's speeches, up will come your dinners.
                                  Joseph H. Choate (1832-1917)

There is an apocryphal story of a suave headwaiter who was being vulgarly abused by a none-too-literate patron. He waited patiently until the man was finished:

My position, sir, does not allow me to argue with you. But if it ever came to a choice of weapons, I should choose grammar.
                                  Anonymous

Writer Randolph Churchill went into hospital to have a lung removed, and his friends sighed with relief when they learned that it was not malignant. All save one —

A typical triumph of modern science to find the only part of Randolph that was not malignant and remove it.
                                  Evelyn Waugh (1903-1966) on
                                  Randolph Churchill

Quite unjustifiably, women have been less noted than men for their finesse at verbal swordplay. One acerbic exception was Margot Asquith, wife of the British prime minister. On her first visit to Hollywood she was introduced to femme fatale Jean Harlow, who asked her about the pronunciation of her name:

No, the t *is silent — as in Harlow.*
Margot Asquith (1864-1945)

Her other sallies tended to make the faint-hearted cringe:

He could not see a belt without hitting below it.
On David Lloyd George

Sir Stafford has a brilliant mind until it is made up.
On Sir Stafford Cripps

Very clever, but his brains go to his head.
On F. E. Smith

The trouble with Lord Birkenhead is that he is so un-Christlike.
On F. E. Smith

His modesty amounts to a deformity.
On her husband, Herbert Asquith

She's as tough as an ox. She'll be turned into Bovril when she dies.
Margot Asquith (1864-1945)

Not everyone appreciated Lady Asquith. Although it was denied, it was generally assumed that a widely circulated poem was composed in her honor:

The haggard cheek, the hungering eye,
The poisoned words that wildly fly,
The famished face, the fevered hand, —
Who slights the worthiest in the land,
Sneers at the just, contemns the brave,
And blackens goodness in its grave. . . .
Malignant-lipped, unkind, unsweet;
Past all example indiscreet.
Who half makes love to you today,
Tomorrow gives her guest away.
William Watson

It was left to Dorothy Parker to have the last word—

The affair between Margot Asquith and Margot Asquith will live as one of the prettiest love stories in all literature.
Dorothy Parker (1893-1967)

Another celebrated harridan was the daughter of President Teddy Roosevelt. "Princess Alice" grew up to be a sharp-tongued lady:

He looks as if he had been weaned on a pickle.
On Calvin Coolidge

The little man on the wedding cake.
On Thomas E. Dewey

One-third Eleanor and two-thirds mush.
On Franklin D. Roosevelt

Eleanor is a Trojan mare.
On Eleanor Roosevelt

Alice Roosevelt Longworth (1893-1967)

and legend had it that her basic philosophy of life was embroidered on a cushion in her drawing room:

If you can't say anything good about somebody, sit right down here beside me.
Alice Roosevelt Longworth (1893-1967)

Yet another crotchety wit, this time a male, was W. S. Gilbert, the verbal half of the sparkling musical team. Neither Gilbert nor his partner thought much of the other:

He is like a man who sits on a stove and then complains that his backside is burning.
Sir William Schwenck Gilbert (1836-1911) on Sir Arthur Sullivan

Another week's rehearsal with WSG & I should have gone raving mad. I had already ordered some straw for my hair.
Sir Arthur Sullivan (1842-1900)
on Sir William Schwenck Gilbert

Sullivan's frustration with rehearsals was justified. Gilbert was renowned as a martinet who would permit no tampering:

173

GILBERT & SULLIVAN

ACTOR: *Look here, sir, I will not be bullied! I know my lines.*
GILBERT: *That may be, but you don't know mine.*

Tact with actors was completely out of Gilbert's line. To the perspiring star of a first-night production, he remarked:

Your skin has been acting at any rate.
To Sir Herbert Beerbohm Tree

And when a prima donna of the day sat down heavily, managing to miss the chair:

Very good, very good. I always thought you would make an impression on the stage one day.
To Henrietta Hodson

As the lyrics to his comic operas attest, Gilbert could seldom resist a play on words. Asked by a patently unmusical woman whether Bach was still composing:

No madam; he's decomposing.
On Johann Sebastian Bach

Gilbert had no great love for the clergy, and one day was appalled to find himself in a room full of clerical collars:

I feel like a lion in a den of Daniels.

When a theater manager praised to the skies an actress with whom he had a rather more than fraternal relationship:

That fellow is blowing his own strumpet.

Perhaps Gilbert's opinion of his fellow man is best summed up by his comment on an old friend:

No one can have a higher opinion of him than I have — and I think he is a dirty little beast.
Sir William Schwenck Gilbert (1836-1911)

The great verbal sallies — or at least those we hear about — are usually directed against politicians, writers, artists — those very much in the public eye. But all sorts and conditions have been the targets of boos and catcalls. Military leaders have frequently irritated their friends and allies:

The greatest cross I have to bear is the Cross of Lorraine.
Winston Churchill (1874-1965)
on Charles de Gaulle

An improbable creature, like a human giraffe, sniffing down his nostrils at mortals beneath his gaze.
Richard Wilson, Lord Moran (b. 1924) on Charles de Gaulle

175

and when they are public heroes, they can be difficult to endure:

In defeat unbeatable, in victory unbearable.
Winston Churchill (1874-1965)
on Bernard L. Montgomery

There is nothing new in this. In the United States, veteran army men after the Civil War were incensed when Adolphus Greely was made a general. He had spent much time as an Arctic explorer, suffering terrible hardships, but had little experience with troops:

He never commanded more than ten men in his life — and he ate three of them.
General Weston on Adolphus W. Greely

In another field, the pretensions of scholars and men of learning have often been open to ridicule. A famous master of Balliol College at Oxford was the victim of a popular parody:

First come I; my name is Jowett.
There's no knowledge but I know it.
I am Master of this College:
And what I don't know isn't knowledge.
H. C. Beeching (1859-1919) on Benjamin Jowett

and another, more recent, "engaged scholar" found his antiwar activities disapproved of:

If I were the Prince of Peace I should choose a less provocative ambassador.
A. E. Housman (1859-1936) on Bertrand Russell

Even distinguished scientists have found that their discoveries are not always appreciated:

Sir Humphrey Davy
Abominated gravy.
He lived in the odium
Of having discovered sodium.

E. C. Bentley (1875-1956) on Humphrey Davy

For some reason, symphony conductors have frequently been noted for the sharp points on their batons. Sir Thomas Beecham's pithy remarks were famous — to a tone-deaf choir:

If you will make a point of singing "All we, like sheep, have gone astray" with a little less satisfaction, we shall meet the aesthetical as well as the theological requirements.

Sir Thomas Beecham (1879-1961)

and, with barely muted sarcasm, on the occasion of his seventieth birthday. As the messages of congratulations were read, he muttered:

What, nothing from Mozart?

Sir Thomas Beecham (1879-1961)

Mozart would have had a hard time matching his ego:

I am not the greatest conductor in this country. On the other hand I'm better than any damned foreigner.

Sir Thomas Beecham (1879-1961)

Beecham was not really all that impressed with his contemporaries and rivals:

A glorified bandmaster!

Sir Thomas Beecham (1879-1961) on Arturo Toscanini

177

and they tended to return the compliment:

He conducted like a dancing dervish.
> Sir John Barbirolli (1899-1970)
> on Sir Thomas Beecham

Barbirolli himself inspired no mean awe amongst his players. One of these, paying a parking fine, explained:

I prefer to face the wrath of the police rather than the wrath of Sir John Barbirolli.
> Anonymous orchestra member
> on Sir John Barbirolli

Meanwhile, across the pond, the ferocious New York maestro had his own threats to keep the musicians in line:

After I die, I shall return to earth as a gatekeeper of a bordello and I won't let any of you — not a one of you — enter.
> Arturo Toscanini (1867-1957)

The world of popular entertainment is not so different from the world of classical music. A sardonic director had the right approach to the making of films:

I deny that I said that actors are like cattle. I said they should be treated like cattle.
> Alfred Hitchcock (1899-1980)

Actors' lives in Hollywood do tend to be sheeplike. Careers are dominated by powerful but ungrammatical columnists:

She never avoids phrases like "the reason is because" unless it is impossible not to do so, and she likes her infinitives split.
> Anonymous on Louella Parsons

and by impresarios who like to repeat their last big hit:

Cecil B. de Mille,
Rather against his will,
Was persuaded to leave Moses
Out of "The Wars of the Roses".
Nicholas Bentley (b. 1907) on C. B. de Mille

Even the most mythical of popular entertainers has suffered the slings and arrows of the unappreciative critic:

Mr. Presley has no discernable singing ability. His specialty is rhythm songs which he renders in an undistinguished whine; his phrasing, if it can be called that, consists of the stereotyped variations that go with a beginner's aria in a bathtub. For the ear he is an unutterable bore.... He is a rock-and-roll variation of one of the most standard acts in show business: the virtuoso of the hootchy-kootchy.
Jack Gould (b. 1917) on Elvis
Presley

Some connoisseurs feel that contemporary invective is just not up to scratch. And while it is true that there is nothing particularly memorable, wise, witty or profound in the standard Hollywood wisecrack, the denizens of tinsel town have produced some good lines —

A day away from Tallulah Bankhead is like a month in the country.
Anonymous; on Tallulah Bankhead

When Jack Benny plays the violin, it sounds as if the strings are still back in the cat.
Fred Allen (1894-1956) on Jack Benny

I never forget a face — but in your case I'll make an exception.

I've had a wonderful evening, but this wasn't it.

Groucho Marx (1890-1977)

I am free of all prejudice. I hate everyone equally.

I always keep a supply of stimulant handy in case I see a snake — which I also keep handy.

W. C. Fields (1880-1946)

I don't have to look up my family tree, because I know that I'm the sap.

Fred Allen (1894-1956) on himself

And, on one occasion at least, a great line:

Please accept my resignation. I don't want to belong to any club that will accept me as a member.

Groucho Marx (1890-1977)

More even than in the entertainment world, waspishness and backbiting are traditional in literary circles, and the tradition goes back a surprisingly long way. A thirteenth-century Italian poet was victimized by subsequent nitpickers:

A Methodist parson in Bedlam.

Horace Walpole (1717-1797) on Dante

A hyena that wrote poetry in tombs.

Friedrich Nietzsche (1844-1900) on Dante

In the volatile world of Elizabethan England, writers were particularly prone to voice delicate criticisms of one another's work:

180

He can raile (what mad Bedlam cannot raile?) but the favour of his railing, is grosely fell, and smelleth noysomly of the pumps, or a nastier thing.... His jestes [are] but the dregges of common scurrilitie ... like old pickle herring: his lustiest verdure, but rank ordure, not be named in Civilitie, or Rhetorique.

> Gabriel Harvey (1545-1630) on Thomas Nashe

It seems that the Elizabethans set an example that later writers have been loath to abandon:

He was an instance that a complete genius and a complete rogue can be formed before a man is of age.

> Horace Walpole (1717-1797) on
> Thomas Chatterton

Bulwer-Lytton I detest. He is the very pimple of the age's humbug.

> Nathaniel Hawthorne (1804-1864) on Edward Bulwer-Lytton

He never wrote an invitation to dinner without an eye to posterity.

> Benjamin Disraeli (1804-1881) on Edward Bulwer-Lytton

On Waterloo's ensanguined plain
Lie tens of thousands of the slain;
But none, by sabre or by shot,
Fell half so flat as Walter Scott.

> Thomas, Lord Erskine (1750-
> 1823) on Sir Walter Scott's *The Field of Waterloo*

Some authors seem naturally to draw fire around their heads. Bernard Shaw delighted in being a gadfly, but his contemporaries showed no hesitation in prodding back:

George Too Shaw To Be Good.

> Dylan Thomas (1914-1953)

That noisiest of old cocks.

Wyndham Lewis (1884-1957)

Too much gas-bag.

D. H. Lawrence (1885-1930) on Bernard Shaw

Some of them detected a streak of puritanism beneath Shaw's thick skin:

His brain is a half-inch layer of champagne poured over a bucket of Methodist near-beer.

Benjamin de Casseres

The first man to have cut a swathe through the theatre and left it strewn with virgins.

Frank Harris (1856-1931) on Bernard Shaw

but the most common complaint was simply that he talked too much:

When you were quite a little boy somebody ought to have said "hush" just once.

Mrs. Patrick Campbell (1865-1940) to Bernard Shaw

Relationships between writers have tended to combine friendship, envy, and emnity in equal portions. Few have been anxious to restrain the critical spirit:

He is conscious of being decrepit and forgetful, but not of being a bore.

Evelyn Waugh (1903-1966) on Hilaire Belloc

He would not blow his nose without moralising on conditions in the handkerchief industry.

Cyril Connolly (1903-1975) on
George Orwell

Chesterton is like a vile scum on a pond. . . . All his slop!
> Ezra Pound (1895-1972) on G. K.
> Chesterton

Things could get particularly sticky when husband and wife both followed a literary bent:

Mr. Fitzgerald — I believe that is how he spells his name — seems to believe that plagiarism begins at home.
> Zelda Fitzgerald (1900-1957) on husband F. Scott Fitzgerald

and in close-knit literary circles, where everyone knew and gossiped about everyone else, almost nothing was beyond the pale. Inevitably, some members came in for special attention — Arnold Bennett, whose fascination with money was a byword:

Bennett — sort of pig in clover.
> D. H. Lawrence (1885-1930)

Nickel cash-register Bennett.
> Ezra Pound (1895-1972)

The Hitler of the book racket.
> Wyndham Lewis (1884-1957) on Arnold Bennett

the trendy Max Beerbohm:

He has the most remarkable and seductive genius — and I should say about the smallest in the world.
> Lytton Strachey (1880-1932)

He is a shallow, affected, self-conscious fribble.
> Vita Sackville-West

Tell me, when you are alone with Max, does he take off his face and reveal his mask?
> Oscar Wilde (1854-1900) on Max Beerbohm

and the quixotic Gertrude Stein, whose elusive prose brought
out the metaphor in others:

What an old covered-wagon she is!
F. Scott Fitzgerald (1896-1940)

*Gertrude Stein's prose is a cold, black suet-pudding. We can
represent it as a cold suet-roll of fabulously reptilian length.
Cut it at any point, it is . . . the same heavy, sticky, opaque mass
all through, and all along.*
Wyndham Lewis (1884-1957) on Gertrude Stein

George Moore — he who told without kissing — was a favorite
victim of his comrades:

George Moore is always conducting his education in public.
Oscar Wilde (1854-1900)

That old pink petulant walrus.
Henry Channon

He leads his readers to the latrine and locks them in.
Oscar Wilde (1854-1900) on George Moore

Moore was quite capable of fighting back, when he cared to:

*Oscar Wilde's talent seems to me essentially rootless, something
growing in a glass in a little water.*
George Moore (1852-1933) on
Oscar Wilde

and in his autobiography, pretentiously titled *Ave Atque Vale,* he
gave a verbal drubbing to one of his former professors in Dublin.
The old Latin scholar sniffed scornfully:

184

Moore is one of those folks who think that "Atque" was a Roman centurion.
Robert Yelverton Tyrrell (1844-1914) on George Moore

Novelist Ford Madox Ford, the "animated adenoid," was another favorite target. For his part, he enjoyed the sport himself:

Conrad spent a day finding the mot juste, *and then killed it.*
Ford Madox Ford (1873-1939) on Joseph Conrad

but he certainly got as good as he gave:

Master, mammoth mumbler.
Robert Lowell (1917-1977)

His mind was like a Roquefort cheese, so ripe that it was palpably falling to pieces.
Van Wyck Brooks (1886-1963)

Freud Madox Fraud.
Osbert Sitwell (1892-1969) on Ford Madox Ford

Perhaps the comments of female literati on their fellow writers have a little more subtlety:

Pale, marmoreal Eliot was there last week, like a chapped office boy on a high stool, with a cold in his head.
Virginia Woolf (1882-1941) on T. S. Eliot

All raw, uncooked, protesting.
Virginia Woolf (1882-1941) on Aldous Huxley

DAME EDITH SITWELL

I thought nothing of her writing. I considered her a "beautiful little knitter."

Edith Sitwell (1887-1964) on Virginia Woolf

Mr. Lawrence looked like a plaster gnome on a stone toadstool in some suburban garden.... He looked as if he had just returned from spending an uncomfortable night in a very dark cave.

Edith Sitwell (1887-1964) on D. H. Lawrence

but this does not prevent sharp elbows or underhand blows. Although this novelist and painter was clearly beloved by all, it took a woman to finish him off:

I do not think I have ever seen a nastier-looking man. . . .
Under the black hat, when I had first seen them, the eyes had
been those of an unsuccessful rapist.
Ernest Hemingway (1899-1961)
on Wyndham Lewis

A buffalo in wolf's clothing.
Robert Ross on Wyndham Lewis

Mr. Lewis's pictures appeared . . . to have been painted by a
mailed fist in a cotton glove.
Edith Sitwell (1887-1964) on Wyndham Lewis

Edith . . . is a bad loser. When worsted in argument, she throws
Queensbury Rules to the winds. She once called me Percy.
Percy Wyndham Lewis (1884-
1957) on Edith Sitwell

It took unfeeling outsiders, however, to put the discussion into
perspective:

The Sitwells belong to the history of publicity rather than of
poetry.
F. R. Leavis (1895-1978)

So you've been reviewing Edith Sitwell's latest piece of virgin
dung, have you? Isn't she a poisonous thing of a woman, lying,
concealing, flipping, plagiarising, misquoting, and being as
clever a crooked literary publicist as ever.
Dylan Thomas (1914-1953) on Edith Sitwell

Even more than writers, politicians expect, and get, a constant
barrage of public criticism. Powerful presidents are not immune.
Teddy Roosevelt had many a run-in with the financial powers-
that-be, and he was hated in the stock exchanges. When he de-

187

parted on a well-publicized safari to Africa, a sign appeared on the New York trading floor:

Wall Street Expects Every Lion To Do Its Duty.
Anonymous

Roosevelt was a fanatic about the simplification of English spelling — an enthusiasm which permitted one New York paper to applaud his retirement from office with a parting shot:

THRU!
Anonymous; on Theodore Roosevelt

Other U.S. presidents have fielded a variety of caustic comments:

To nominate Grover Cleveland would be to march through a slaughterhouse into an open grave.
Henry Watterson on Grover Cleveland

He had a bungalow mind.
Woodrow Wilson (1856-1924) on Warren G. Harding

A fat Coolidge.
H. L. Mencken (1880-1956) on Herbert Hoover

A chameleon on plaid.
Herbert Hoover (1874-1964) on Franklin D. Roosevelt

The croon of croons.
H. L. Mencken (1880-1956) on Franklin D. Roosevelt

He looks like the guy in a science fiction movie who is the first to see the Creature.
David Frye on Gerald Ford

Every prospective U.S. president has to endure an arduous election campaign, but some don't appear to mind losing favor with at least part of the public:

A hippie is someone who looks like Tarzan, walks like Jane and smells like Cheeta.
                                   Ronald Reagan (b. 1911) on losing the hippie vote

Abraham Lincoln's presidential opponent had to overcome apparently insuperable difficulties:

Douglas never can be president, Sir. No, Sir; Douglas never can be president, Sir. His legs are too short, Sir. His coat, like a cow's tail, hangs too near the ground, Sir.
                                   Thomas Hart Benton (1782-1858)
                                   on Stephen A. Douglas

but in any case, Lincoln appeared to have his measure:

I did keep a grocery, and I did sell cotton, candles and cigars, and sometimes whiskey; but I remember in those days Mr. Douglas was one of my best customers. Many a time have I stood on one side of the counter and sold whiskey to Mr. Douglas on the other side, but the difference between us now is this: I have left my side of the counter, but Mr. Douglas still sticks to his as tenaciously as ever.
                                   Abraham Lincoln (1809-1865) on
                                   Stephen A. Douglas

Not just presidents, but royal princes are on the receiving end of criticism. It comes hard, however, from one's nearest and dearest:

His intellect is no more use than a pistol packed in the bottom of a trunk if one were attacked in the robber-infested Apennines.
                                   Prince Albert (1819-1861) on his son, later Edward VII

189

Even minor and long-forgotten American politicians have had to face the hoots and gibes of their contemporaries:

Damn John Jay! Damn every one that won't damn John Jay! Damn every one that won't put lights in his windows and sit up all night damning John Jay!!!
> Anonymous; on John Jay, 1794

Mr. Ames's friends treated his memory as they did his body.
> John Quincy Adams (1767-1848)
> on Fisher Ames

A becurled and perfumed grandee gazed at by the gallery-gapers.
> James G. Blaine (1830-1893) on Roscoe Conkling

Wallowing in corruption like a rhinoceros in an African pool.
> E. L. Godkin (1831-1902) on James G. Blaine

No man in our annals has filled so large a space and left it so empty.
> Charles Edward Russell on James G. Blaine

In Great Britain, things were no better. Complain, complain, complain:

He was oppressed by metaphor, dislocated by parentheses, and debilitated by amplification.
> Samuel Parr (1747-1825) on a speech by Edmund Burke

His temper naturally morose, has become licentiously peevish. Crossed in his Cabinet, he insults the House of Lords, and plagues the most eminent of his colleagues with the crabbed malice of a maundering witch.
> Benjamin Disraeli (1804-1881)
> on the earl of Aberdeen

Dangerous as an enemy, untrustworthy as a friend, but fatal as a colleague.

Sir Hercules Robinson on Joseph Chamberlain

He has the mind and manners of a clothes brush.

Harold Nicholson (1886-1968) on
Austen Chamberlain

D. is a very weak-minded fellow I am afraid, and, like the feather pillow, bears the marks of the last person who has sat on him! I hear he is called in London "genial Judas"!

General Douglas Haig (1861-1928) on the 17th earl of Derby

Black and wicked and with only a nodding acquaintance with the truth.

Lady Cunard on Herbert Asquith

His fame endures; we shall not forget
The name of Baldwin until we're out of debt.

Kensal Green on Stanley Baldwin

Every time Mr. Macmillan comes back from abroad Mr. Butler goes to the airport and grips him warmly by the throat.
Harold Wilson (b. 1916) on Harold Macmillan and R.A.B. Butler

In the face of all this political Billingsgate, one has only two options — to follow the dictates of a master political strategist:

Never complain. Never explain. Get even.

Robert F. Kennedy (1925-1968)

or, like Matthew Arnold, to take refuge in philosophy:

When Abraham Lincoln was murdered
The one thing that interested Matthew Arnold

191

Was that the assassin shouted in Latin
As he leaped from the stage.
This convinced Matthew
There was still hope for America.
Christopher Morley (1890-1957)

You slawzy poodle, you tike,
You crapulous puddering pipsqueak!
Christopher Fry (b. 1907) *The*
Lady's Not for Burning

Get out, you blazing ass!
Gabble o' the goose. Don't bugaboo-baby me!
C. S. Calverley (1831-1884) *The*
Cock and the Bull

Shut your fat gob, you nasty little pile of wombat's do's!
Monty Python's Flying Circus, "A Bad Conversation with the Queen"

192

The Poisoned Pen

TALLEYRAND

Long before that monument to inefficiency, the modern post office, became the institution everybody loves to hate, the letter had established itself as the perfect vehicle for the expression of malicious wit. What better opportunity to polish a well-turned phrase while preserving the appearance of spontaneity, to jab with a pointed sentence or cascade paragraphs of scorn on one's hapless victim? And for us, the unintended readers of this uncivil correspondence, there is the guilty enjoyment of the voyeur — as we intrude on the privacy and eavesdrop on the less than worthy thoughts of others.

The letter's effectiveness as a personal weapon has undoubtedly declined since the formidable days of Junius and Dr. Johnson. Their lengthy and studied insolence is no longer in vogue. Today, our greatest admiration is reserved for those who can condense their wit into a few brief phrases. A classic, if apocryphal, example is this plea from an English schoolboy to his father:

S.O.S. L.S.D. R.S.V.P.
Anonymous

It is perhaps necessary, in a decimal age, to add that the second set of letters refers to pounds, shillings and pence.

The puckish wit of the French statesman Talleyrand is demonstrated in this pair of letters sent, with the briefest of intervals, to a beautiful widow; the first on the death of her husband:

Hélas, madame!

the second on her remarriage:

Ho! ho! madame!
Charles Maurice de Talleyrand-Périgord (1754-1838)

When a clergyman serving under a 19th-century English bishop requested a leave of absence to travel to the Holy Land, the good shepherd's reply went directly to the point:

Dear Sir:
Go to Jericho.
Yours,
A.W.R.
Anthony William Thorold (1825-1895)

Bernard Shaw once achieved an unaccustomed brevity in responding to a collector of social scalps. Receiving a card with the inscription:

Lady ———— will be at home on Thursday between four and six o'clock.

Shaw returned the invitation with the handwritten notation:

Mr. Bernard Shaw likewise.
Bernard Shaw (1856-1950)

The writer Hilaire Belloc was at one time engaged by the London *Morning Post,* where he frustrated his employers by his infrequent appearances and his proprietary air. One can only picture the scene which led to this little cry of pent-up fury from his editor:

March 23, 1909

Dear Belloc,
I owe you an apology for the way I shouted at you this afternoon; but please don't, *on your rare and unexpected visits to the office (about which I shall say more on another occasion) stand in my door and wag a finger at me when I am engaged on private and difficult business.*
Yours,
F.W.
Fabian Ware (1869-1949) to Hilaire Belloc

Paternal pride is a noble feeling. But the father of a shockingly irreverent satirist was willing to put it to one side to spare his own feelings:

May 29, 1872

Dear Sam,
I shall take your advice and not read your book. It would probably pain me and not benefit you.
   Your affectionate father,
T. BUTLER

Canon T. Butler to Samuel Butler

Unrequested and unwanted gifts always create the problem of acknowledgment:

Many thanks for your book; I shall lose no time in reading it.
Benjamin Disraeli (1804-1881)

or the well-meaning friend who unloads her latest bargain —

I thank you for the snip of cloth, commonly called a pattern. At present I have two coats and but one back. If at any time hereafter I should find myself possessed of fewer coats and more backs, it will be of use to me.
William Cowper (1731-1800); letter to Lady Hesketh

Other unsolicited presentations seem to cry out for a clever response. A bottle of fruit, for instance, preserved in brandy:

DEAR AUNT,
A thousand thanks for your kind gift. I appreciate the cherries immensely, not so much for themselves as for the spirit in which they are sent.
Anonymous

or the bounties of summer sent to a not ungrateful but ironical canon:

What is real piety? What is true attachment to the Church? How are these fine feelings best evinced? The answer is plain: by sending strawberries to a clergyman. Many thanks.
                                    Sydney Smith (1771-1845)

The preservation of sanity and temper from time to time demands the short, sharp retort. During one school crisis the head of Haileybury College was inundated with well-meaning advice from parents and friends. In self-defense he printed up a postcard — an idea that anyone obliged to court public opinion today might well duplicate:

DEAR SIR,
I am obliged by your opinions, and retain my own.
                                    Anonymous

But then, friendship is a fragile thing at best. Did it survive, one wonders, this little interchange between a political candidate and his near neighbor?

                                    February 28, 1820

MY DEAR SIR,
In times like the present, it is impossible to allow private feelings to take the place of a public sense of duty. I think your conduct as dangerous in Parliament as it is in your own county. Were you my own brother, therefore, I could not give you my support.
            THOMAS LIDDELL

MY DEAR SIR THOMAS,
In answer to your letter, I beg to say that I feel gratitude for your frankness, compassion for your fears, little dread of your opposition, and no want of your support. — I am, etc.,
        J. G. LAMBTON

Certainly there was a relish in the twist with which a Philadelphia kite-flyer put an end to an even longer friendship:

You are a member of Parliament, and one of that majority which has doomed my country to destruction. — You have begun to burn our towns, and murder our people. — Look upon your hands! They are stained with the blood of your relations! — You and I were long friends: — You are now my enemy, — and I am
    Yours
    B. FRANKLIN

                    Benjamin Franklin (1706-1790);
                    letter to William Strahan

Both friendships and family ties are often strained by finances, and when money-talk finds its way into personal letters acrimony is almost sure to ensue. Long before he declined to read his son's book, Canon Butler had expressed the exact worth of young Sam's talents:

                                    May 9, 1859
Dear Sam:
If you choose to act in utter contradiction of our judgment and wishes, and that before having acquired the slightest knowledge of your powers which I see you overrate in other points, you can of course act as you like. But I think it right to tell you that not one sixpence will you receive from me after your Michaelmas payment till you come to your senses. ..
                  Canon T. Butler to Samuel Butler

Letters appealing for money run the risk of being unsympathetically received. The samaritan who requested a donation to pay off the mortgage of the Duke Street Chapel got more than he bargained for:

SIR,

I am scornfully amused at your appeal to me, of all people in the world the precisely least likely to give you a farthing! My first word to all men and boys who care to hear me is "Don't get into debt. Starve and go to heaven — but don't borrow. Try first begging — I don't mind if it's really needful — stealing! But don't buy things you can't pay for!" And of all manner of debtors pious people building churches they can't pay for, are the most detestable nonsense to me. Can't you preach and pray behind the hedges — or in a sandpit — or a coalhole first? And of all manner of churches thus idiotically built, iron churches are the damnablest to me. And of all the sects and believers in any ruling spirit — Hindoos, Turks, Feather Idolaters, and Mumbo Jumbo, Log and Fire Worshippers — who want churches, your modern English Evangelical sect is the most absurd, and entirely objectionable and unendurable to me!

All which they might very easily have found out from my books — any other sort of sect would! — before bothering me to write it to them. Ever, nevertheless, and in all this saying, your faithful servant

JOHN RUSKIN

John Ruskin (1819-1900)

Ruskin's strictures against borrowing could well have been heeded by these two friends. Apparently the effort to recover a loan had gone past the subtle stage:

Sept 4 [1925]

I believe I am corrupting you: for when I first unmasked you — pulling the rock away and there you were, so to speak — you behaved in a very dignified and suitable way, didn't you?

... But I think you are deteriorating.... you are growing indecent.

You say, let the original arrangement stand: but where's the cheque, old boy? Where's the esteemed favour that that arrangement arranged for? ... If you can't evacuate the six pounds, and if you are as constipated about a thing like that as you are about your food, well, tell me so, and there will be an end of the matter. Don't for the love of Mike get ill about it. But unless there is some natural obstruction of that sort, instead of saying let the arrangement stand, do something; sit down at your desk, draw out your cheque-book, write me a nice polite little note saying you are sorry there has been any trouble, close your eyes, hold your breath, and write six — *and there you will be straight with me, at all events.*

Wyndham Lewis (1884-1957);
letter to O. R. Drey

Avoiding the borrower's touch has always called forth the utmost in ingenuity:

DEAR SON,
I am in prison for debt; come and assist your loving mother.
E. FOOTE

DEAR MOTHER,
So am I; which prevents his duty being paid to his loving mother. —Your affectionate son,
SAMUEL FOOTE
P.S. —*I have sent my attorney to assist you; in the meantime let us hope for better days.*

Samuel Foote (1720-1777)

MY DEAR SCROPE,
Lend me two hundred pounds. The banks are shut and all my

200

money is in the three per cents. It shall be repaid to-morrow morning. —*Yours,*
GEORGE BRUMMEL

MY DEAR GEORGE,
'Tis very unfortunate, but all my money is in the three per cents. —*Yours,*
S. DAVIES

George (Beau) Brummel (1778-1840)

'BEAU' BRUMMEL

and so has the writing of collection letters. The resolutely eccentric American painter James McNeill Whistler habitually gave his paintings such exotic titles as *Arrangement in Black and White* or *Harmony in Grey and Green*. The secretary of his London club, despairing of a long-overdue bill, finally hit the mark:

Dear Mr. Whistler:
It is not a Nocturne in Purple *or a* Symphony in Blue and Grey
we are after, but an Arrangement in Gold and Silver.
Anonymous

Whistler paid up, of course.

Violations of the code of proper and civilized conduct have had a curious ability to arouse a most uncivilized ire. Oscar Wilde, usually so urbane in conversation, fired off a genuinely outraged letter when a journalist included some of his personal conversations in a book of anecdotes. The thing just wasn't gentlemanly!

I was not asking you to do me a favour; I was asserting my right to prevent my name being in any way associated with a book that . . . I consider extremely vulgar and offensive. No one has the right to make one godfather to a dirty baby against one's will. . . . I should be sorry to think that any Cambridge man could be wilfully guilty of such conduct, conduct which combines the inaccuracy of the eavesdropper with the method of the blackmailer.
Oscar Wilde (1854-1900); letter to Herbert Vivian

William Thackeray took similar umbrage when an acquaintance retailed versions of his conversations in a series of "Literary Talk" columns. The offense was compounded by having been committed in that most holy of sanctums — a gentleman's club:

We meet at a Club, where, before you were born I believe, I and other gentlemen have been in the habit of talking without any idea that our conversation would supply paragraphs for professional vendors of "Literary Talk"; and I don't remember that out of that Club I have ever exchanged six words with you. Allow me to inform you that the talk which you have heard there is not intended for newspaper remark; and to beg — as I have a right to do — that you will refrain from printing comments upon my private conversations; that you will forego discussions, however blundering, upon my private affairs; and that you will henceforth please to consider any question of my personal truth and sincerity as quite out of the province of your criticism.

    W. M. THACKERAY.
William Makepeace Thackeray (1811-1863); letter to Edmund Yates

The gentleman's club had a code of behavior all its own. One of the most celebrated libel cases of the 1920s also centered around a letter from a club. The rumpus began when a young writer resurrected an old slur on the morals of the long-dead William Ewart Gladstone:

Gladstone . . . founded the great tradition . . . in public to speak the language of the highest and strictest principle, and in private to pursue and possess every sort of woman.
             Peter Wright on William Ewart Gladstone

The next Earl Gladstone and his brother, sons of the Grand Old Man, rose to the defense with commendable directness:

Mr. Peter Wright,
Your garbage about Mr. Gladstone in "Portraits and Criticisms" has come to our knowledge. You are a liar. Because you slander a dead man, you are a coward. Because you think the public will accept invention from such as you, you are a fool.

    GLADSTONE.

I associate myself with this letter.

    H. N. GLADSTONE.

Unrepentant, Wright reproached the brothers for their unparliamentary zeal:

My Lord, —
I am in receipt of your Lordship's outburst dated July 22nd. . . .
My views are unshaken even by the impact of your Lordship's controversial language, which, if I may say so without impoliteness, must rather have been acquired by practice in your Lordship's pantry than by the exercise of your Lordship's talents for debate in the House of Lords.
PETER E. WRIGHT.
The Bath Club, Dover Street, W.

It was that postscript that did him in. To calumniate the dead was unsporting; to do it from the Bath Club — unthinkable! His Lordship appealed to the secretary:

Dear Wilson Taylor,
Mr. Peter Wright appears to be a member of the Bath Club. In a book he made a foul charge against my father. He elaborated this in a letter to the Nation. . . . *He wrote on Bath Club notepaper. . . . It seems to me that this is a matter for the Committee.*
Sincerely yours,
GLADSTONE

My Dear Wilson Taylor,
. . . I wrote to you because I was so indignant that the fellow was sheltering in my old Club, which, for my brother, myself and my wife becomes uninhabitable so long as it is polluted by his presence. . . . By his baseless attacks on my father he has wantonly and deliberately insulted the fellow members of his Club.
GLADSTONE

Lord Gladstone (1854-1930)

Wm. E.
GLADSTONE

The committee, on cue, promptly expelled the cad, who there-
upon sued for restitution and for libel. He was restored to the
again polluted club but lost his libel suit ignominiously. Gladstone at last was vindicated — and the Bath Club had played its
role.

All of which nonsense is much at odds with the dignified
reproaches made to the citizens of Birmingham by one of the
pioneers of modern science. At the height of popular feeling
against the French Revolution, the mob had sacked his house:

July 19, 1791

MY LATE TOWNSMEN AND NEIGHBOURS,
*You have destroyed the most truly valuable and useful appa-
ratus of philosophical instruments that perhaps any individual,*

in this or any other country, was ever possessed of . . . . You have destroyed the Library corresponding to that apparatus . . . But what I feel far more, you have destroyed manuscripts which have been the result of the laborious study of many years, and which I shall never be able to recompense; and this has been done to one who never did, or imagined, you any harm.

In this business we are the sheep and you the wolves. We will preserve our character and hope you will change yours. At all events we return you blessings for curses, and hope that you shall soon return to that industry and those sober manners for which the inhabitants of Birmingham were formerly distinguished.

Yours faithfully,

J. PRIESTLEY

Joseph Priestley (1733-1804); letter to the inhabitants of Birmingham

Twentieth-century letter writers have shown much less of this "more in sorrow than in anger" approach. There is a distinct tone of "you're another" as America's most caustic columnist taxes a rival for his thin skin:

You are far, far better on the give than on the take. No man in American history has denounced more different people than you have, or in more violent terms, and yet no man that I can recall complains more bitterly when he happens to be hit. Why not stop your caterwauling for a while, and try to play the game according to the rules?

H. L. Mencken (1880-1956); letter to Upton Sinclair

and as a famous drama critic hotly disputes the meaning of a word with a popular lyricist:

206

Listen, you contumacious rat, don't throw your dreary tomes at me. I'll give you an elegant dinner ... and sing to you between the courses if you can produce one writer or speaker, with an ear for the English language ... who uses "disinterested" in the sense you are now trying to bolster up ... a ghetto barbarism I had previously thought confined to the vocabularies of Ben Hecht and Jed Harris.

Alexander Woollcott (1887-1943); letter to Ira Gershwin

Modern literary gentlemen have even been known to slash, unsuccessfully, at each other's jugulars:

August 21, 1919
... Although I recognize you as a man of wit I realize it is not of the spontaneous order. There is nothing of the Whistler about you.... You, like the mills of God, grind slow, and I might add, grind exceedingly small....

I am ... at a loss to explain how you should so far forget your pose as to express [your feelings] in such a laborious and boorish fashion, exposing to my astonished understanding the indication of a nature so calculating, petty, malicious and uncivilized, in short so strangely sub-human, as to realize almost the popular estimate of your character...

Paul Nash (1889-1946); letter to Wyndham Lewis

August 25 [1919]
I am distressed to find ... that I should have driven such a dignified gentleman into the lamentable lapse of a series of tu quoques. *But I might have known that would happen! I sprinkle myself with a few ashes.... I must leave you for the present to ruminate on ... how back-biting, shittiness and every*

mean practice is the specialty of your "sub-human" and bestial
enemies (whom Yaveh confound!).
Wyndham Lewis (1884-1957) letter to Paul Nash

A relatively feeble slanging-match, compared to those engaged in long ago by such combatants as Daniel O'Connell and Benjamin Disraeli. Admirers at first, the two fell out when the young writer abandoned his Radical beginnings and ran as a Tory politician. The old Irishman castigated Disraeli's race and his motives. The younger man challenged O'Connell's long-suffering son to a duel, which was refused; Disraeli turned to more pointed weapons:

London, May 6 *[1835]*

Mr. O'Connell:
Although you have long placed yourself out of the pale of civilization, still I am one who will not be insulted, even by a Yahoo, without chastising it. When I read ... your virulent attacks upon myself, and that your son was at the same moment paying the penalty of similar virulence to another individual on whom you had dropped your filth ... I called upon your son to reassume his vicarious office of yielding satisfaction for his shrinking sire. But it seems that gentleman declines the consequences of your libertine harangues. ... Listen, then, to me.

If it had been possible for you to act like a gentleman, you would have hesitated before you made your foul and insolent comments ... I admire your scurrilous allusions to my origin. It is quite clear that the "hereditary bondman" has already forgotten the clank of his fetter. ... With regard to your taunts as to my want of success in my election contests, permit me to remind you that I had nothing to appeal to but the good sense of the people ... My pecuniary resources, too, were limited; I am not one of those public beggars that we see swarming with their obtrusive boxes in the chapels of your creed, nor am

208

I in possession of a princely revenue wrung from a starving race of fanatical slaves....

We shall meet at Philippi; and ... I will seize the first opportunity of inflicting upon you a castigation which will make you at the same time remember and repent the insults that you have lavished upon

BENJAMIN DISRAELI

Benjamin Disraeli (1804-1881)

Disraeli's nemesis, Gladstone — that unintentional instigator of the Bath Club affair — did not have to wait for death to be insulted by post. Upset at changes the Grand Old Man was proposing to the Welsh church, an anonymous correspondent compressed onto one small postcard all the verbosity of her race, unleavened by the slightest touch of Christian charity:

Cannes, March 15, 1893
Far away from my native Land, my bitter indignation as a Welshwoman prompts me to reproach you, you bad, wicked, false, treacherous Old Man! ... You have no conscience, but I pray that God may even yet give you one that will sorely smart and trouble you before you die. You pretend to be religious, you old hypocrite! that you may more successfully pander to the evil passions of the lowest and most ignorant of the Welsh people.... You think you will shine in History, but it will be a notoriety similar to that of Nero. I see someone pays you the unintentional compliment of comparing you to Pontius Pilate, and I am sorry, for Pilate, though a political time-server, was, with all his faults, a very respectable man in comparison with you.... You are certainly cleverer. So also is your lord and master the Devil. And I cannot regard it as sinful to hate and despise you, any more than it is sinful to abhor Him. So with full measure of contempt and detestation, accept these compliments from

"A DAUGHTER OF OLD WALES"   Anonymous; letter to William
Ewart Gladstone

Enough! Far better the terse, civilized restraint, the ironic gibe at family pretensions, of a John Bright, taunted by a Tory politician named Smith:

> *He may not know that he is ignorant, but he cannot be ig-norant that he lies.... I think the speaker was named Smith. He is a discredit to the numerous family of that name.*
> John Bright (1811-1899)

Bravado, in letter writing as elsewhere, has its own reward. This rogue's effrontery clearly amused Charles II, but there is a glint of steel in the monarch's reply:

KING CHARLES, —
One of your subjects, the other night, robbed me of forty pounds, for which I robbed another of the same sum, who has inhumanly sent me to Newgate, and he swears I shall be hanged; therefore, for your own sake, save my life, or you will lose one of the best seamen in your navy.
JACK SKIFTON

JACK SKIFTON —
For this time I'll save thee from the gallows; but if hereafter thou art guilty of the like, by —— I'll have thee hanged, though the best seaman in my navy. — Thine,
CHARLES REX
Charles II (1630-1685)

The gentle Charles Lamb was one of the greatest of English letter writers. Like many otherwise innoffensive people, he was never happier than when making critical fun of others — in this case his sister:

210

DEAR MISS H., —

Mary has such an invincible reluctance to any epistolary exertion, that I am sparing her a mortification by taking the pen from her. The plain truth is, she writes such a pimping, mean, detestable hand, that she is ashamed at the formation of her letters. There is an essential poverty and abjectness in the frame of them. They look like begging letters.... Her figures, 1, 2, 3, 4, &c., ... are not figures, but figurantes; and the combined posse go staggering up and down shameless, as drunkards in the day-time. It is no better when she rules her paper.... A sort of unnatural parallel lines, that are perpetually threatening to meet; which, you know, is quite contrary to Euclid. Her very blots are not bold like this, [HERE A BOLD BLOT] but poor smears, half left in and half scratched out, with another smear left in their place.... I don't think she can make a corkscrew if she tried.

Charles Lamb (1775-1834) to Miss Hutchinson

Of course, critical comment is hardly confined to the purely personal letter, as any business can attest. Some customers will complain about anything. In these times of relative religious tolerance it is hard to imagine the depth of feeling that inspired this querulous complaint:

January 8, 1908

DEAR SIRS, —

I am sorry to return the Drawers, which are a trifle too small round the waist. At the expense of being considered bigoted, to tell you the truth, I do not like the Brand, although the material is excellent in quality.

The man whose likeness appears, "WOLSEY," was one under whom poor Protestants writhed, and although you may say this is a small matter and of no importance, it indicates the

211

Firm at least allowing such to go forth in these critical times is at least careless, if not genuine Roman Catholics, and a Feather will indicate which way the wind blows.

Again the buttons would be far better of linen instead of pearl. Please to send me others.

Believe me, Yours faithfully.

Anonymous

The character reference, beloved of prospective employers, provides a heaven-sent opportunity for ambiguous phrases and damning with faint praise. Sometimes, however, the applicant does himself in, as does this eternally optimistic but all too honest father, eager to secure an "interest" for his young hopeful:

To the Honourable Board of Directors of the East India Co.

GENTLEMEN,

I have a parcel of fine boys, but not much cash to provide for them. I had intended my eldest son for the Church, but I find he is more likely to kick a church down than support it. I sent him to the University, but he could not submit himself to the college rules, and, on being reproved by his tutors, he took it up in the light of an affair of honour, and threatened to call them to account for it. All my plans for his welfare being thus disconcerted, I asked him if he had formed any for himself; he replied, he meant to go to India. I then inquired if he had any interest, at which question he looked somewhat foolish, and replied in the negative. Now, gentlemen, I know no more of you than you do of me. I therefore may appear to you not much wiser than my son. I can only say that he is of Welsh extraction for many generations, and, as my first-born, I flatter myself, has not degenerated. He is six feet high, of an athletic make, and bold and intrepid as a lion. If you like to see him I will equip him as a gentleman, and, I am, Gentlemen, etc.

Anonymous letter to the East India Company

212

One may imagine with what guarded enthusiasm John Company regarded the advent of this lion-like, church-bashing young Taffy.

A character reference was also the genesis of a remarkable early-Victorian correspondence which demonstrated, had it been doubted, that women are equally adept as men at pointed incivility. The initial letter was innocent enough:

Lady Seymour presents her compliments to Lady Shuckburgh, and would be obliged to her for the character of Mary Stedman, who states that she lived twelve months, and still is, in Lady Shuckburgh's establishment. Can Mary Stedman cook plain dishes well? make bread? and is she honest, good-tempered, sober, willing, and cleanly? Lady Seymour would also like to know the reason why she leaves Lady Shuckburgh's service? Direct, under cover to Lord Seymour, Maiden Bradley.

Lady Jane Seymour was the granddaughter of Richard Brinsley Sheridan, and had all the great dramatist's sparkle. Some time earlier, at a bizarre pseudo-medieval tournament led by Louis Napoleon, she had been chosen "Queen of Beauty" — a triumph that apparently galled at least one rival. To Lady Seymour's domestic inquiries was returned a disdainful reply:

Lady Shuckburgh presents her compliments to Lady Seymour. Her ladyship's note, dated October 28, only reached her yesterday, November 3. Lady Shuckburgh was unacquainted with the name of the kitchen-maid until mentioned by Lady Seymour, as it is her custom neither to apply for or give characters to any of the under servants, this being always done by the housekeeper, Mrs. Couch — and this was well known to the young woman; therefore Lady Shuckburgh is surprised at her referring any lady to her for a character. Lady Shuckburgh having a professed cook, as well as a housekeeper, in her

establishment, it is not very likely she herself should know any-
thing of the abilities or merits of the under servants; therefore
she is unable to answer Lady Seymour's note. Lady Shuckburgh
cannot imagine Mary Stedman to be capable of cooking for
any except the servants'-hall table.

Lady Seymour was too much her grandfather's granddaughter to swallow such hoity-toity high-handedness. A casual misspelling reveals the true Sheridan touch:

Lady Seymour presents her compliments to Lady Shuckburgh,
and begs she will order her housekeeper, Mrs. Pouch, to send
the girl's character without delay; otherwise another young
woman will be sought for elsewhere, as Lady Seymour's chil-
dren cannot remain without their dinners because Lady Shuck-
burgh, keeping a "professed cook and a housekeeper", thinks
a knowledge of the details of her establishment beneath her
notice. Lady Seymour understands from Stedman that, in ad-
dition to her other talents, she was actually capable of dressing
food fit for the little Shuckburghs to partake of when hungry.

Appended to this missive was a pen and ink cartoon of the three Shuckburgh children, with large heads and cauliflower wigs, slavering over a chop prepared by a grinning Mary Stedman, while their mother hovered in dismay.

This was too much for offended dignity. The attempted squelch-by-proxy, when it came, managed to reveal the true cause of Lady Shuckburgh's pique:

MADAM,
Lady Shuckburgh has directed me to acquaint you that she
declines answering your note, the vulgarity of which is beneath
contempt; and although it may be the characteristic of the
Sheridans to be vulgar, coarse, and witty, it is not that of a

214

"lady", unless she happens to have been born in a garret and bred in a kitchen. Mary Stedman informs me that your ladyship does not keep either a cook or a housekeeper, and that you only require a girl who can cook a mutton chop. If so, I apprehend that Mary Stedman, or any other scullion, will be found fully equal to cook for or manage the establishment of the Queen of Beauty. I am, your Ladyship, &c.,
    ELIZABETH COUCH *(not Pouch).*

The correspondence was at an end. One supposes that Stedman was soon cooking mutton chops for small descendents of Sheridan, and that the honors, if any, went to the Queen of Beauty.

MY DEAR SIR,
I have read your play.
    Oh, my dear Sir.
        Yours Faithfully
            HERBERT BEERBOHM TREE

Sir Herbert Beerbohm Tree
(1853-1917) to a would-be
dramatist

Three Curmudgeons and a Canon

CURMUDGEON: *A testy, grumpy, gruff, irascible man; a grouch.*

W.S. LANDOR

Wm. COBBETT

DUKE of WELLINGTON

We all know them. People whose instinct is to criticize; who are quick to give and take offense; whose habitual frame of mind is irritation — people who can lay claim to the name curmudgeon. But only occasionally does someone arise whose breathtaking bloody-mindedness and captivating cantankerousness combine with an inspired ability to put them into words. For lovers of malicious wit, true curmudgeons have such an irresistible charm that they deserve to be immortalized in some left-handed Hall of Fame.

Three contumacious curmudgeons, now largely forgotten, have a particular appeal today. Although they were contemporaries, they were very different men. William Cobbett was a politician, pamphleteer and journalist who crusaded against social and political injustice in language so extreme that today it is difficult to credit. The duke of Wellington was the victorious general of the Battle of Waterloo. As curt and blunt as Cobbett was long-winded, Wellington was a staunch defender of the status quo who did not know the meaning of the word tact and who never suffered a fool in his life. Walter Savage Landor was a much less public figure, a fierce old literary gentleman with a formidable temper, who never missed a chance to take arms against a sea of real or imagined foes.

Like us, these curmudgeons lived through a time of momentous and bewildering change. They experienced the American and French revolutions, the twenty long years of the Napoleonic wars, and the transformation of England from a rural to an industrial nation. And although their reactions to these events were totally different, they shared the supreme egotism of knowing that they were always right, and their fellow men always wrong.

The Watchdog
William Cobbett (1763-1835)

The very quintessence of a curmudgeon was William Cobbett. Cobbett was an extraordinary man — a soldier, a crusading journalist, a rabble-rousing Radical politician, a teacher, an agricultural experimenter, and always a man of violent and eccentric opinions. As prickly as his pseudonym, "Peter Porcupine," implied, he was one of those people who are naturally "anti."

Cobbett looked like John Bull and acted like Don Quixote, riding the length and breadth of England tilting at the windmills of injustice. In words as vigorous and powerful as they were intemperate, he flailed away at men in power and out of power, at new opinions and old ideas, never reckoning the consequences and never minding where his incendiary packages landed. Civilized and dignified men found him a bit heavy-handed:

> *A Philistine with six fingers on every hand and on every foot six toes, four and twenty in number: a Philistine the shaft of whose spear is like a weaver's beam.*
> Matthew Arnold (1822-1888) on
> William Cobbett

Cobbett was like a bomb bursting in air — spectacular but with few lasting results. He had exploded on the scene as a young pamphleteer horrified by the ideas behind the American and French revolutions:

> *How Thomas Paine gets a living now, or what brothel he inhabits I know not.... Like Judas he will be remembered by*

posterity; men will learn to express all that is base, malignant, treacherous, unnatural and blasphemous by the single monosyllable — Paine.

On Thomas Paine

In one of the many 180-degree turns that marked his career, Cobbett later became a passionate advocate of many of those same ideas. To atone for his attacks on Paine, he removed the English-born revolutionary's mortal remains from the unhallowed ground where they were buried in America, with some hazy notion of erecting a memorial in England. The plan fizzled; the bones lay forgotten for many years in a suitcase in Cobbett's house, and on his death they disappeared forever. The whole bizarre episode provided a field day for the doggerel writers:

Cobbett, through all his life a cheat,
Yet as a rogue was incomplete,
For now to prove a finished knave
To dupe and trick, he robs a grave.

Anonymous, 1818

In digging up your bones, Tom Paine,
Will. Cobbett has done well:
You visit him on earth again,
He'll visit you in Hell.

Lord Byron (1788-1824)

Cobbett was at bottom a romantic conservative fighting desperately to restore the overidealized rural England he loved. He abhorred the corrupt political "System" which, of course, was responsible for every social evil. And he despised the new financial powers and the rise of the stock exchange, which he christened with typical venom:

The Muckworm is no longer a creeping thing: it rears its head

219

*aloft, and makes the haughty Borough Lords sneak about in
holes and corners.*

Cobbett also vented his wrath on the new type of country squires,
who cared nothing for their workers or the poor:

*These incomparable cowards; these wretched slaves; these dirty
creatures who call themselves country gentlemen, deserve ten
times as much as they have yet had to suffer. . . .
      The foul, the stinking, the carrion baseness, of the fellows . . .*

He deplored the growing gulf between rich and poor in England,
and contrasted the plight of the laborer with the life-style of the
social-climbing rich farmer:

*A fox-hunting horse; polished boots; a spanking trot to market;
a "Get out of the way or by G-d I'll ride over you" to every
poor devil upon the road; wine at his dinner; a servant (and
sometimes in* livery) *to wait at his table; a painted lady for a
wife; sons aping the young 'squires and lords; a house
crammed up with sofas, pianos, and all sorts of fooleries.*

To Cobbett, cities were a blot on the earth — London he always
referred to as "the Great Wen." One day he passed through
Cheltenham, a fashionable spa:

*Which is what they call a "watering-place"; that is to say, a
place to which East India plunderers, West India floggers, English tax-gorgers, together with gluttons, drunkards, and de-
bauchees of all descriptions, female as well as male, resort, at
the suggestion of silently laughing quacks, in the hope of getting
rid of the bodily consequences of their manifold sins and in-
iquities. . . . To places like this come all that is knavish and all
that is foolish and all that is base; gamesters, pick-pockets, and*

harlots; young wife-hunters in search of rich and ugly old women, and young husband-hunters in search of rich and wrinkled or half-rotten men, the former resolutely bent, be the means what they may, to give the latter heirs to their lands and tenements.

On Cheltenham

Cobbett's greatest charm was his diversity. Never single-minded, he tended to ride off in all directions at once. A discussion of political reform would suddenly become a diatribe against classical authors:

Those base, servile, self-degraded wretches, Virgil and Horace.

A crawling and disgusting parasite, a base scoundrel, and pandar to unnatural passion.

On Virgil

or an attack on the nation's literary giants:

Indeed, the whole of Milton's poem is such barbarous trash, so outrageously offensive to reason and to common sense that one is naturally led to wonder how it can have been tolerated by a people, amongst whom astronomy, navigation, and chemistry are understood.

On *Paradise Lost*

or a vilification of the fashionable musicians who infested the cities:

Squeaking wretches who have consumed this year two or three thousand quarters of corn.

The singers and their crew are not only useless in themselves, but spread about at large their contagious effeminacy.

On Italian singers in London

Many of his notions were nothing if not eccentric. He damned tea as a pallid and evil beverage that would weaken England's moral fiber:

The gossip of the tea table is no bad preparatory school for the brothel.

and never missed an opportunity to denounce that most despicable of all plants, the humble potato. In the good old days, such rubbish had not polluted the table of the farm worker; but now

his beer and his bread and meat are . . . exchanged for the cat-lap of the tea-kettle, taxed to more than three-fourths of its prime cost, and for the cold and heartless diet of the potato plant.

Ranging far and wide, Cobbett could work up the most astonishing head of steam against historical figures who had been dead for over 200 years:

A name which deserves to be held in everlasting execration; a name which we could not pronounce without almost doubting of the justice of God, were it not for our knowledge of the fact, that the cold-blooded, most perfidious, most impious, most blasphemous caitiff expired at last, amidst those flames which he himself had been the chief cause of kindling.
On Archbishop Thomas Cranmer

and against literary sacred cows. Cobbett had supreme confidence in his ability to set all things right:

Dr. Dread-Devil . . . said that there were no trees in Scotland. I wonder how they managed to take him around without

letting him see trees. I suppose that lick-spittle Boswell, or Mrs. Piozzi, tied a bandage over his eyes when he went over the country which I have been over. I shall sweep away all this bundle of lies.
On Samuel Johnson

His contemporaries fared no better. Pitt, for instance, the chief exponent of "the System":

The great snorting bawler.
On William Pitt

or a passing chief minister:

What will now be said to this cowardly crowing of pompous chanticleer upon his own dunghill?
On Henry Addington, Viscount Sidmouth

or an execrable monarch:

As a son, as a husband, as a father, and especially as an advisor of young men, I deem it my duty to say that, on a review of his whole life, I can find no one good thing to speak of, in either the conduct or character of this king.
On George IV

When it came to women, there was a curious streak of Mrs. Grundy in Cobbett. S-E-X was a word not to be mentioned. What is one to make, for instance, of his opposition to wet-nurses, who allow a new mother:

... to hasten back, unbridled and undisfigured, to those enjoyments, to have an eagerness for which, a really delicate woman will shudder at the thought of being suspected.

or even to the remarriage of a widow, who has:

> ... a second time *undergone that surrender, to which nothing but the most ardent affection could ever reconcile a chaste and delicate woman.*

Cobbett could never distinguish between people and their ideas, and he translated his disapproval of Malthus's theories into a violent hatred of the man:

> *Parson,*
> *I have during my life, detested many men; but never any one so much as you. ... Priests have, in all ages, been remarkable for cool and deliberate and unrelenting cruelty; but it seems to be reserved for the Church of England to produce one who has a just claim to the atrocious pre-eminence. No assemblage of words can give an appropriate designation of you; and therefore, as being the single word which best suits the character of such a man, I call you Parson, which, amongst other meanings, includes that of Boroughmonger's Tool.*
> To Thomas Malthus

Although he did become an MP, Cobbett achieved less than many had expected. It took an observant foreigner to explain why:

> *He is a chained house-dog who falls with equal fury on every one whom he does not know, often bites the best friend of the house, barks incessantly, and just because of this incessantness of his barking cannot get listened to, even when he barks at an actual thief. Therefore the distinguished thieves who plunder England do not think it necessary to throw the growling Cobbett a bone to stop his mouth. This makes the dog furiously savage, and he shows all his hungry teeth. Poor old Cobbett! England's watch-dog!*
> Heinrich Heine (1797-1856) on William Cobbett

The Iron Duke
The duke of Wellington
(1769-1852)

A minor but memorable figure in the ranks of curmudgeonry was Arthur Wellesley, duke of Wellington. Victor of Waterloo, prime minister of Great Britain, field marshal of the army, the Iron Duke was in his way a legendary and epic character. Crusty, testy and irascible he certainly was, but unlike most of his fellow curmudgeons he was a man of remarkably few words, and his gruff terseness became his trademark. Speaking of another prime minister, he once barked:

> *I have no small talk and Peel has no manners.*
> On Robert Peel

Permitting no liberties and given to calling a spade a spade, the duke was nothing if not blunt. When a lady with more familiarity than good sense inquired whether he had been surprised to discover he had won the Battle of Waterloo, he replied frigidly:

> *By God! not half as much surprised as I am right now, mum.*

At the height of his considerable fame, which he accepted as only his due, a stranger approached him in the street:

STRANGER: *Mr. Robinson, I believe?*
WELLINGTON: *Sir, if you believe that you'll believe anything.*

225

Having in one instance against his will accepted the arm of a passerby in crossing the street, he listened with impatience as the stranger burbled his pleasure in helping the victor of Waterloo, then grunted:

Don't be a damned fool

and turned on his heel. The old warrior had no illusions about the value of military glory:

There is nothing worse than a defeat except a victory.

and even fewer about the kind of spectacular heroism appreciated by the crowd:

There is nothing on earth so stupid as a gallant officer.

Perverse as always, Wellington heaped scorn on the elite troops of the army, the cavalry.

The only thing that they can be relied on to do is to gallop too far and too fast.

When a detachment of fresh young officers arrived at his camp during the Peninsular War, he eyed them with something less than enthusiasm:

I don't know what effect they will have upon the enemy, but by God, they frighten me!

Much as he disapproved of all his troops, Wellington despised the victorious army of Waterloo most:

The scum of the earth — they have enlisted for drink, that is the simple truth.

The most infamous army I ever commanded.

Utter unflappability was one of the duke's most visible qualities. On the field of Waterloo he rode with his second-in-command as the musket balls whistled by:

LORD UXBRIDGE: *By God, there goes my leg!*
WELLINGTON: *By God, so it does.*

and while he respected his chief opponent, he found one of his qualities regrettable:

He is no gentleman.
On Napoleon Bonaparte

The French, in turn, didn't think much of Wellington:

Waterloo was a battle of the first rank won by a captain of the second.
Victor Hugo on the duke of Wellington

Congenitally opposed to anything newfangled, he had no patience with modern trends in music. As ambassador in Vienna he suffered through a performance of Beethoven's *The Battle of Vitoria,* and when asked by a Russian diplomat whether the music resembled the real battle:

By God, no, if it had been, I should have run away myself.
On Beethoven's *The Battle of Vitoria*

Wellington's gradual involvement in politics threw him into contact with the reigning House of Hanover. Apparently oblivious of his own habitual profanity, he disapproved strongly of the dissolute prince regent:

By God, you never saw such a figure in your life as he is. Then he speaks and swears so like old Falstaff, that damn me if I am not ashamed to walk into a room with him.

On the prince regent (later
George IV)

The prince's wife, later Queen Caroline, was also a favorite with the duke:

CAROLINE: *You see how punctual I am, Duke; I am even before my time.*
WELLINGTON: *That, your majesty, is not punctuality.*

Caroline, accused by her profligate husband of many and flagrant infidelities, became the centre of a violent public controversy. At its height she was urged by a pompous preacher to "Go, and sin no more." Popular doggerel took up the cry:

Most Gracious Queen, we thee implore
To go away and sin no more,
But if that effort be too great,
To go away at any rate.

Anonymous; on Queen Caroline

The London mob supported the queen, so Wellington, typically, opted for the king. Driving through the City, he was set upon by a gaggle of workmen who refused to let him pass until he pronounced "God Save the Queen." The duke shrugged:

Well, gentlemen, since you will have it so — "God save the Queen"; and may all your wives be like her!

The duke of Wellington (1769-1852) on Queen Caroline

The Iron Duke went on to become one of the most reactionary prime ministers in history, inveighing against the popular agitation for political change. He was appalled by the members of the newly reformed House of Commons:

I never saw so many shocking bad hats in my life.

Nevertheless, he was a shrewd and sometimes cynical politician. Of a singularly uninspired minister he noted:

Oh! He is a very good bridge for rats to run over.
On William Huskisson

The duke spent so much time away from home that he became a stranger to his family. His children were something of a trial to him, particularly the eldest, Lord Douro, who was extraordinarily like him:

There is only one caricature of me that has ever caused me annoyance: Douro.

The Iron Duke never had the least doubt of his own self-worth or place in the world. The French marshals, chagrined at their defeat by an inferior, turned their backs on him at Vienna. To a sympathetic onlooker, the duke smiled his frosty smile:

Madam, I have seen their backs before.
The duke of Wellington (1769-1852)

The Old Lion
Walter Savage Landor
(1775-1864)

A curmudgeon of a character very different from either Cobbett or Wellington was the aptly named Walter Savage Landor. Landor is remembered now chiefly as a minor poet and essayist, a classicist who wrote much of his poetry in Latin and translated it into English and an accomplished stylist whose balanced, periodic sentences are reminiscent of Dr. Johnson's. But in his own day he was the Old Lion, celebrated for his growl. Aristocratic, snobbish, serenely self-confident and self-important, Landor was one of those people who see personal affront everywhere. A lifelong series of wrangles with one adversary after another culminated in his virtual exile from England in late middle-age as the result of a libel suit. He was possessed of an extravagant and ungovernable temper which tended to explode in all directions. The unpredictable fallout might descend anywhere — on the luckless architect of his Welsh farmhouse:

> *The earth contains no race of human beings so totally vile and worthless as the Welsh ... I have expended in labour, within three years, eight thousand pounds amongst them, and yet they treat me as their greatest enemy...*
>
> Letter to Robert Southey

— or on the head of his not undeserving publisher, John Taylor, who had scissored some typically controversial passages from a Landor manuscript:

> *His first villany ... instigated me to throw my fourth volume, in its imperfect state, into the fire, and has cost me nine-tenths*

of my fame as a writer. His next villany will entail perhaps a chancery-suit on my children, —for at its commencement I blow my brains out . . . This cures me forever, if I live, of writing what could be published . . . Not a line of any kind shall I leave behind me. My children shall be carefully warned against literature. To fence, to swim, to speak French, are the most they shall learn

Letter to Robert Southey

Landor had a high opinion of himself as a writer and of the supreme importance of writers in general. But he took a jaundiced view of authors themselves, both contemporary and remote — Byron, for instance:

Byron dealt chiefly in felt and furbelow, wavy Damascus daggers, and pocket pistols studded with paste. He threw out frequent and brilliant sparks; but his fire burnt to no purpose; it blazed furiously when it caught muslin, and it hurried many a pretty wearer into an untimely blanket.

On Lord Byron

— and Shakespeare:

Not a single one [of the sonnets] is very admirable. . . . They are hot and pothery: there is much condensation, little delicacy; like raspberry jam without cream, without crust, without bread.

On Shakespeare's sonnets

Never one to overvalue consistency, Landor also castigated those who didn't appreciate Shakespeare enough! An eye witness described the Old Lion in full flight:

During one of the sittings the artist happened to speak enthusiastically about some lines of Ben Jonson, whereupon Mr. Landor, who was seated at the time, bounded from his chair, and began pacing the room and shaking his tightly clenched

231

hands as he thundered out "Ben Jonson! Not another word about him! It makes my blood boil! I haven't patience to hear the fellow's name. A pigmy! an upstart! a presumptuous varlet who dared to be thought more of than Shakespeare was in his day!" "But surely," ventured the artist, "that was not poor Ben Jonson's fault, but the fault of the undiscriminating generation in which they both lived." "Not at all!" roared Landor, his eyeballs becoming bloodshot and his nostrils dilating, "not at all! The fellow should have walled himself up in his own brick and mortar before he had connived at and allowed such sacrilege!" "But!," said I — for the painter could not speak for laughter — "even if Ben Jonson had been able to achieve such a tour de force, I am very certain, Mr. Landor, that Shakespeare would have been the very first to pull down his friend's handiwork and restore him to the world." "No such thing!" rejoined Mr. Landor, turning fiercely upon me; "Shakespeare never wasted his time; and with his woonderful imagination, he'd have known he could have created fifty better."

Lady Bulwer-Lytton (1802-1882)
on Walter Savage Landor

One of Landor's favorite targets was Wordsworth. An early admirer of the Lake poet, Landor soon took umbrage at Wordsworth's egotism and his alleged mistreatment of his fellow poet Robert Southey. Henceforth he seldom missed an opportunity to aim a well-turned metaphor:

The surface of Wordsworth's mind, the poetry, has a good deal of staple about it, and will bear handling; but the inner, the conversational and private, has many coarse intractable dangling threads, fit only for the flockbed equipage of grooms.

On William Wordsworth

Ultrasensitive to criticism himself, Landor inveighed against the literary critics, particularly those of the *Edinburgh Review*. Even the Old Lion was unable to bring much ill nature to bear on the rotund and amiable Sydney Smith:

Humour's pink Primate, Sydney Smith

He reserved the full vigor of his plain speaking for the most visible of the *Review*ers, Henry Brougham, who had long since risen to the eminence of lord chancellor. Vain and ambitious, Brougham had been incautious enough to sue a London paper for libel. Landor fired off a withering denunciation to the editor:

> SIR: *The prosecution with which you are threatened by Lord Brougham might well be expected from every facette of his polygonal character.... In the days when Brougham and his confederates were writers in [the* Edinburgh Review], *more falsehood and malignity marked its pages than any other Journal in the language....*
>
> *What other man within the walls of Parliament, however hasty, rude, and petulant, hath exhibited such manifold instances of bad manners, bad feelings, bad reasonings, bad language, and bad law?*
>
> On Henry, Lord Brougham

Republican in sentiment since the days of his youth, Landor regarded the momentous political events of his time with a cynical and fastidious eye. But when William IV's ministers removed from Coleridge the miserly state pension awarded by George IV, Landor was able to rouse himself to something like his customary level of indignation:

> *George IV, the vilest wretch in Europe, gave him £100 a year, enough, in London, to buy three turnips and half an egg a day. Those men were surely the most dexterous of courtiers,*

who resolved to shew William that his brother was not the vilest, by dashing the half egg and three turnips from the plate of Coleridge. No such action as this is recorded of any administration in the British annals, and I am convinced that there is not a state in Europe, or Asia, in which the paltriest minister of the puniest despot would recommend it.

Landor had once used his gift for deadly doggerel to pin the wings of the Hanoverian Georges; years later he did the same for the British military with his immortal couplet on the Crimean War:

Hail, you indomitable heroes, hail!
Despite of all your generals, ye prevail.

In spite of his irascibility, or because of it, Landor managed to retain a number of fast friends who bomb-proofed themselves against occasional mortar fire and were sometimes even able to return it. Once, when Landor was violently attacking, of all things, the Psalms, Lady Blessington smiled sweetly and cooed:

Do write something better, Mr. Landor.
Marguerite, Countess Blessington
(1789-1849)

Definitely a low blow. After receiving a missive with a pointed invitation, Charles Dickens took a fiendish delight in turning the other cheek:

YOUNG MAN, — *I will not go there if I can help it. I have not the least confidence in the value of your introduction to the Devil. ... If you were the man I took you for ... you would come to Paris and amaze the weak walls of the house I haven't found yet with that steady snore of yours, which I once heard piercing the door of your bedroom in Devonshire Terrace,*

234

reverberating along the bell wire in the hall, so getting outside into the street, playing Aeolian harps among the area railings, and going down the New Road like the blast of a trumpet.

I forgive you your reviling of me: there's a shovelful of live coals for your head — does it burn? And am, with true affection — does it burn now? — Ever yours.

Charles Dickens (1812-1870);
letter to Walter Savage Landor

The rampant Old Lion, capable of instant and extravagant rage, is seen in full roar in what can only be interpreted as a challenge to a duel with a lawyer who had been a conspicuously bad samaritan. The contrast between the triviality of the offense and the formality of the classical style is almost ludicrous. The balanced sentences, the Latin tag, the snobbery, the casual aspersions on his victim's breeding, learning and professional capacity — all are Landor at his most typical:

Permit me, Sir, to recall to your memory your insulting language and violent demeanor of yesterday ... I had just taken refuge from the rain under your verandah, when I heard the following words, uttered with a coarseness and vehemence I had never heard before from any well-dressed man on any occasion. "What do you want here? Be off with you." Until I heard the latter phrase spoken close to me, I did not imagine or suspect that it was addressed to me. On my asking you ... whether it was so, you answered in the affirmative, and still more offensively. I ... reminded you that such language was not usually applied to a gentleman. You expressed a doubt whether I am one. I gave you all the benefit of that doubt, knowing that only a gentleman can judge of one correctly.

But I thought my manner, my language, and my tone, were unexceptionable, and (what you are more capable of appreciating) my dress. It is that in which, during last week, I had visited several of the first families in Cornwall ... in whose

society you will never be admitted, unless (to their sorrow) professionally. . . . In your terms and utterance there was what Cicero calls subrancidum nescio quid *The curate of your parish will explain this to you. . . . I caused no obstruction: I stood several feet from the doorway, and with my back toward it. On my expostulating, you not only repeated the same insolence of expression, but you advanced in a menacing and outrageous attitude.*

There is no great bravery in thus insulting a man of seventy-three, without a cane or whip in his hand: but the man of seventy-three has not yet forgotten, in case of necessity and in a proper time and place, to repel a ruffian and to spurn a coward.

Letter to James Jerwood

Landor could, when he chose, be brief. All his sense of dignity and self-worth is summoned up in this icy rebuke to a political lordling who had cut him dead at Florence; its closing is the essential Walter Savage Landor:

MY LORD, — *Now I am recovering from an illness of several months' duration, aggravated no little by your lordship's rude reception of me at the Cascine, in presence of my family and innumerable Florentines. I must remind you in the gentlest terms of the occurrence.*

We are both of us old men, my lord, and are verging on decrepitude and imbecility. Else my note might be more energetic. I am not unobservant of distinctions. You, by the favour of a Minister, are Marquis of Normanby; I by the grace of God am

WALTER SAVAGE LANDOR.

Walter Savage Landor (1775-
1864); letter to the marquis of
Normanby

236

The Canon of Wit
Sydney Smith (1771-1845)

SYDNEY
SMITH

Periodically there comes along one of those rare souls who tran-
scend their own time — whose brilliance and wit charm every
generation, and who continue to speak in words that seem fresh
and modern. The Reverend Sydney Smith was such a man. He
was the very opposite of a curmudgeon — a high-spirited and
convivial man who never failed to see the essential comedy of
the human condition. Captivating he most certainly was, but not
in the conventional sense. A huge, Falstaffian figure,

he allowed his expansive wit full play as, without malice but with
finely pointed humor and ridicule, he punctured the reputations
of the pompous and assailed the works of the vain and stupid.

In his day, Sydney Smith was acknowledged as the wittiest man
in England. For over forty years he dominated London society
with his exhilarating conversation and the force of his jovial
personality, in spite of the fact that in all that time he was rarely
in the city more than one or two months a year. But there was
much more than this to Sydney Smith. As canon of St. Paul's
Cathedral he reorganized the cathedral's doddering finances. He
was an exemplary country parson and a brilliant preacher. He
was perhaps one of the two or three greatest letter writers the
English language has ever produced. He was cofounder of the
Edinburgh Review, a journal whose influence on four generations
of Englishmen was incalculable. And as a political reformer and
adviser to prime ministers and statesmen, his effect on nineteenth-century English political and social life was greater than
has ever been acknowledged.

The essence of Sydney Smith's wit lay in his imagination. Both
he and his listeners would shake with laughter as, seized with
an idea, he piled one flight of ludicrous fancy on another. He
was informed one day that a young Scot of his acquaintance was
engaged to marry a widow twice his age, whose dimensions
rivaled Sydney's own:

*Going to marry her! Going to marry her! impossible! you mean,
a part of her; he could not marry her all himself. It would be
a case, not of bigamy, but of trigamy; the neighbourhood or
the magistrates should interfere. There is enough of her to
furnish wives for a whole parish. One man marry her! — it is*

monstrous. You might people a colony with her; or give an assembly with her; or perhaps take your morning walks around her, always providing there were frequent resting places, and you are in rude health. I once was rash enough to try walking round her before breakfast, but only got half-way and gave it up exhausted. Or you might read the Riot Act and disperse her; in short, you might do anything with her but marry her.

Less spontaneous but equally typical and ridiculous was Smith's speculation on the metaphysical significance of tropical birds. As with so many of his apparently light-hearted comparisons, the sting is in the tail:

The toucan has an enormous bill, makes a noise like a puppy dog, and lays his eggs in hollow trees. How astonishing are the freaks and fancies of nature! To what purpose, we say, is a bird placed in the woods of Cayenne with a bill a yard long, making noise like a puppy dog, and laying eggs in hollow trees? The toucans, to be sure, might retort, to what purpose were gentlemen in Bond Street created? To what purpose were certain foolish Members of Parliament created? — pestering the House of Commons with their ignorance and folly, and impeding the business of the country? There is no end of such questions. So we will not enter into the metaphysics of the toucan.

Although Smith was celebrated for his wit and humor, it was his tragedy that his enormous talents were never fully utilized because the solemn and serious men in power could not bring themselves to trust him. He was too independent — too irreverent — and just too damned funny!

Sydney Smith's ambition was to be a lawyer, but poverty and his father's insistence drove him into the Church. During a brief stint as a tutor in Edinburgh he helped found the *Edinburgh*

239

Review; afterwards he made something of a splash in London society. But then his finances forced him to accept a twenty-year exile to a poor country-living in the north of England. To a man of Smith's urbanity and gregarious nature, life in the country was akin to the grave:

Whenever I enter a village, straightway I find an ass.

Unlike Cobbett, he had no romantic notions about the virtues of rural society. He dealt too much with the poor to idealize them:

A ploughman marries a ploughwoman because she is plump; generally uses her ill; thinks his children an encumbrance; very often flogs them; and, for sentiment, has nothing more nearly approaching to it than the ideas of broiled bacon and mashed potatoes.

He contemplated with irony the fate of Jean Jacques Rousseau, the prophet of the natural life, condemned to a rural estate by his patroness, Madame d'Epinay:

Among the real inhabitants of the country, the reputation of reading and thinking is fatal to character; and Jean Jacques cursed his own successful eloquence which had sent him from the suppers and flattery of Paris to smell daffodils, watch sparrows, or project idle saliva into the passing stream.

One might have expected such a man to become despondent. But Smith, to the amazement and amusement of his friends, plunged into the agricultural life with vigor, while still finding time to read, keep up a wide correspondence, write vigorously for the *Review,* and captivate London on his brief annual forays.

Smith's tenure in Edinburgh had left him with an exasperated admiration for the Scots. Thereafter he could never resist the opportunity to poke fun at them, and many a letter or article was enlivened by an offhand dig:

> *It requires a surgical operation to get a joke well into a Scotch understanding. Their only idea of wit, or rather that inferior variety of this electric talent which prevails occasionally in the north, and which, under the name of* wut, *is so infinitely distressing to people of good taste, is laughing immoderately at stated intervals.*

> *[Palmerston's] manner when speaking is like a man washing his hands; the Scotch members don't know what he is doing.*

> *That garret of the earth — the knuckle-end of England — that land of Calvin, oat-cakes and sulphur.*

Not that Sydney had any illusions about the national character of his own people:

> *It must be acknowledged that the English are the most disagreeable of all the nations of Europe — more surly and morose, with less disposition to please, to exert themselves for the good of society, to make small sacrifices, and to put themselves out of their way.*

In Paris he was embarrassed by the spectacle of the Ugly Englishman:

> *The house was full of English, who talk loud and seem to care little for other people. This is their characteristic, and a very brutal and barbarous distinction it is.*

Smith knew the Americans only at second remove. Like many an Englishman, he was inclined to undervalue them:

In the four corners of the globe, who reads an American book? or goes to an American play? or looks at an American picture or statue? What does the world yet owe to American physicians or surgeons? .. Who drinks out of American glasses? or eats from American plates? or wears American coats or gowns? or sleeps in American blankets? Finally, under which of the old tyrannical governments of Europe is every sixth man a slave, whom his fellow creatures may buy and sell and torture?

He was distressed by a habit which had been remarked by countless English travelers:

We are terribly afraid that some Americans spit on the floor, even when that floor is covered by good carpets. Now all claims to civilization are suspended till this secretion is otherwise disposed of. No English gentleman has spit upon the floor since the Heptarchy.

Smith had several later altercations with the Americans, and they ultimately retaliated by consistently spelling his name *Sidney*!

Smith was intensely ambitious, but he recognized that his own habits of mind did not mark him for preferment in his profession:

In the Church, if you are not well born, you must be very base or very foolish, or both.

Sydney was neither. In common with many others, he did not hold a high opinion of the average clergyman:

SQUIRE *If I had a son who was an idiot, by Jove, I'd make him a parson!*
SMITH *Very probably; but I see that your father was of a different mind.*

242

The Church of England in the nineteenth century was almost a branch of the civil service, and high clerical appointments were inevitably political. In spite of his significant services to social and political reform, his Whig friends, when they came to power, did not choose to make him a bishop. Sydney was too likely to say what he thought. He was a man of conscience who could not be relied upon to toe the line. He was finally elevated to the position of canon of St. Paul's, but watched lesser men appointed to the bench of bishops.

Smith was deeply disappointed, but the man was incapable of bitterness. He would have been less than human, however, had he not seized every opportunity to tweak the ear of the bishops; sometimes with high seriousness:

> *It is a melancholy thing to see a man, clothed in soft raiment, lodged in a public palace, endowed with a rich portion of the product of other men's industry, using all the influence of his splendid situation, however conscientiously, to deepen the ignorance, and inflame the fury, of his fellow creatures.*

but more often in the tongue-in-cheek style that was his trademark:

> *I must believe in the Apostolic Succession, there being no other way of accounting for the descent of the Bishop of Exeter from Judas Iscariot.*

> *How can a bishop marry? How can he flirt? The most he can say is, "I will meet you in the vestry after service."*

Sydney Smith was intensely involved in the social and political movements of his day — always on the side of reform and progress. His views on many issues seem so timeless that we can still identify with them — on the overkill of taxation, for instance:

Taxes upon every article which enters into the mouth, or covers the back, or is placed under the foot — taxes upon everything which is pleasant to see, hear, feel, smell or taste — taxes on everything on earth, and the waters under the earth ... The schoolboy whips his taxed top, the beardless youth manages his taxed horse, with a taxed bridle, on a taxed road — and the dying Englishman, pouring his medicine, which has paid 7 per cent, into a spoon that has paid 15 per cent, flings himself back on his chintz bed, which has paid 22 per cent, and expires into the arms of an apothecary who has paid a licence of a hundred pounds for the privilege of putting him to death.

or on the evils of colonization. Smith used India as an example:

If the Bible is universally diffused in Hindustan, what must be the astonishment of the natives to find that we are forbidden to rob, murder and steal; we who, in fifty years, have extended our empire ... over the whole peninsula ... and exemplified in our public conduct every crime of which human nature is capable. What matchless impudence to follow up such practice with such precepts! If we have common prudence, let us keep the gospel at home, and tell them that Machiavelli is our prophet, and the god of the Manicheans our god.

All his life Smith suffered from the realization that he was mis-understood — that his great good humor was taken for buffoo-nery and his prodigious talents undervalued:

Smug Sydney.
                                        Lord Byron (1788-1824)

A more profligate parson I never met.
                                        George IV (1762-1830)

The truth is that Sydney Smith is naturally coarse, and a lover of scurrilous language.

John Ward, earl of Dudley (1781-1833)

He was too much of a jack-pudding.

Henry Brougham (1778-1868) on
Sydney Smith

But since he had the delightful quality of refusing to take himself too seriously, Smith remained an eloquent, high-spirited dinner guest. More and more he was forced to deal with the duties of being a social lion:

MY DEAR DICKENS,
I accept your obliging invitation conditionally. If I am invited by any man of greater genius than yourself, or one by whose works I have been more completely interested, I will repudiate you, and dine with the more splendid phenomenon of the two.

It speaks volumes for Charles Dickens's breadth of character that he maintained warm friendships with two such different beings as Landor and Smith.

Turning down invitations was a frequent Smith problem; either from necessity:

Dear Longman, I can't accept your invitation, for my house is full of country cousins. I wish they were once removed.

or from disinclination. Opera bored him to tears:

Thy servant is threescore-and-ten years old; can he hear the sound of singing men and singing women? A Canon at the Opera! Where have you lived? In what habitations of the heathen? I thank you, shuddering; and am ever your unseducible friend.

and he had little interest in protracted popular entertainments:

Music for such a length of time (unless under sentence of a jury) I will not submit to. What pleasure is there in pleasure if quantity is not attended to as well as quality?

I never go to plays, and should not care (except for the amusement of others) if there was no theatre in the whole world; it is an art intended only for amusement, and it never amuses me.

London was Sydney's milieu — London, where he was "surrounded by a Caspian sea of soup" — although the delights of the capital carried some associated drawbacks:

He who drinks a tumbler of London water has literally in his stomach more animated beings than there are men, women and children on the face of the globe.

London had conviviality: good talk, good food, cheerful fires and lights. On one occasion, Samuel Rogers experimented at a dinner party with placing the candles high on the walls, to show off his paintings. Sydney was asked how he liked the effect:

Not at all; above there is a blaze of light, and below nothing but darkness and gnashing of teeth.

So powerful was Sydney's spell that people remembered not so much what he had said, but how much they had laughed. Mrs. Siddons, the tragedian who was so dramatic that Sydney said she stabbed the potatoes at dinner, actually went into a convulsion while dining with Smith and had to be helped from the table. Such occurrences were apparently not unusual. Fortunately some of the bon mots have survived:

Go where you will, Mrs. Grote; do what you please. I have the most perfect confidence in your indiscretion

Harrowgate is the most heaven-forgotten country under the sun. When I saw it there were only nine mangy fir trees there; and even they all leaned away from it.

Heat ma'am? It was so dreadful here that I found there was nothing left for it but to take off my flesh and sit in my bones.

When I first saw Brighton pavilion, I thought that St. Paul's Cathedral had come down and pupped.

The departure of the Wise Men from the East seems to have been on a more extensive scale than is generally supposed, for no one of that description seems to have been left behind.

Smith's many life-long friendships withstood a constant barrage of gibes. Totally devoid of malice, these quips were nonetheless frequently wicked. Samuel Rogers had pretensions to being a poet:

Rogers is not very well.... Don't you know he has produced a couplet? When he is delivered of a couplet, with infinite labour and pain, he takes to his bed, has straw laid down, the knocker tied up, expects his friends to call and make enquiries, and the answer at the door invariably is "Mr. Rogers and his little couplet are as well as can be expected." When he produces an Alexandrine he keeps to his bed a day longer.
On Samuel Rogers

Sydney punctured the scholarly pretensions of one of the few bishops with whom he was on amiable terms:

I have written to Maltby ... that you have peculiar opinions about the preterpluperfect tense; and this, I know, will bring him directly, for that tense has always occasioned him much uneasiness, though he has appeared to the world cheerful and serene.

On Bishop Maltby

and made constant fun of the gourmet propensities of Henry Luttrell:

Mr. Luttrell is going gently down-hill, trusting that the cookery in another planet may be at least as good as in this; but not without apprehensions that for misconduct here he may be sentenced to a thousand years of tough mutton, or condemned to a little eternity of family dinners.

On Henry Luttrell

Cobbett's bête noire, Malthus, who advocated population control, was a frequent visitor:

Philosopher Malthus came here last week. I got an agreeable party for him of unmarried people. There was only one lady who had a child; but he is a good-natured man, and if there are no appearances of approaching fertility, is civil to every lady.

On Thomas Robert Malthus

Sydney greatly admired Thomas Macaulay, considering him one of the best minds in the country. Still, this did not deter him from endless jokes about Macaulay's tendency to non-stop talking:

I wish I could write like you. I could write an Inferno, *and I would put Macaulay amongst a number of disputants and gag him.*

I spent a horrid, horrid night! I dreamt I was chained to a rock and being talked to death by Harriet Martineau and Macaulay.
On Thomas Babington Macaulay

The devious and egotistical Henry Brougham was one of the *Review*'s cofounders; Smith's enthusiasm for him waned with the years. Seeing him ride by in the strange crested carriage to which he gave his name, Sydney remarked

There goes a carriage with a B outside and a wasp within.
On Henry Brougham

Assessing a Brougham article for the *Review*, Smith allowed that

It is long yet vigorous, like the penis of a jackass.

As he grew older, Sydney consoled himself with thoughts of another and better world:

We shall meet again in another planet, cured of all our defects. Rogers will be less irritable; Macaulay more silent; Hallam will assent; Jeffrey will speak slower; Bobus will be just as he is; and I shall be more respectful to the upper clergy.
Sydney Smith (1771-1845)

Somehow, one rather doubts it.

Of Graves, of Worms, and Epitaphs

Let's talk of graves, of worms, and epitaphs.
William Shakespeare (1564-1616) *Richard II*

In lapidary inscriptions a man is not upon oath.
Samuel Johnson (1709-1784)

Wm.
SHAKESPEARE

De mortuis nihil nisi bonum — Speak nothing but good of the dead. One of mankind's oldest taboos, and still one of its most faithfully observed. And it has never been enough merely to speak no evil. A plain statement of facts, let alone a touch of irreverence, is regarded as a shocking and insulting liberty. Cynics, of course, have always taken a rather skeptical view of the fulsome obituary that celebrates the virtues and glosses over the defects of the departed:

Friend, in your epitaph I'm grieved
So very much is said:
One-half will never be believed.
The other never read.
Anonymous

and have devised pointed little aphorisms to express their disenchantment:

EPITAPH: *An inscription on a tomb, showing that virtues acquired by death have a retroactive effect.*
Ambrose Bierce (1842-1914)

Epitaph: A belated advertisement for a line of goods that has been permanently discontinued.
Irvin S. Cobb (1876-1944)

But the taboo is a strong one. Our own age, having replaced sex with death as the ultimate obscenity, continues to toe the line. Still, there have always been squads of largely anonymous badmouths who delight in shocking their fellows by speaking, if not evil, at least no good of their deceased contemporaries. And most of us, with a slightly guilty relish, are only too happy to listen.

Speaking ill of the dead has sometimes involved other perils as well. As late as 1824 libel suits and imprisonment were all too real prospects. But this danger was laid to rest later in the century when a prominent Cardiff merchant went to his dubious reward. A critical solicitor of the town suggested a fitting inscription for the inevitable statue:

> *In honour of John Batchelor, a native of Newport, who in early life left his country for his country's good; who on his return devoted his life and energies to setting class against class, a traitor to the Crown, a reviler of the aristocracy, a hater of the clergy, a panderer to the multitude; who as first chairman of the Cardiff School Board, squandered funds to which he did not contribute; who is sincerely mourned by unpaid creditors to the amount of £50,000; who at the close of a wasted and misspent life died a pauper, this monument, to the eternal disgrace of Cardiff, is erected by sympathetic Radicals.*
> OWE NO MAN ANYTHING.
>
> Anonymous; suggested epitaph 1887

Mr. Batchelor's pained relations promptly sued for libel, but the case was lost, and the principle firmly established that one cannot libel the dead.

There were those who had never doubted it. Often the easiest way to malign the dead involved sticking strictly to the facts:

> *Here lies the body of Richard Hind,*
> *Who was neither ingenious, sober, nor kind.*
>
> Anonymous; *Webb's Epitaphs* 1775

with sometimes a little editorial comment thrown in:

> *Here Lies*
> *Ezekial Aikle*
> *Aged 102*
> *The Good*
> *Die Young*
>
> Anonymous; East Dalhousie, N.S.

252

A well-known atheist was determined to perpetuate his opinions from his own tombstone:

Haine Haint
> Arthur Haine; Vancouver, B.C., cemetery

while a London journalist, succinct and to the point, managed to evaluate his friend's life in three words:

Hotten
Rotten
Forgotten
> George Augustus Henry Sala on John Camden Hotten

At first glance the composer of this epitaph seems to have been unreasonably critical —

Lord, she is Thin
> Anonymous; Annapolis County, N.S., graveyard

but a closer look reveals that some latter-day proofreader has supplied the final *e* inadvertently omitted by the carver.

The necessity to find praiseworthy qualities where few exist has proved too much of a strain for some, who resort to indiscriminate name-dropping and damning with faint praise:

Here lies the body of
Lady O'Looney,
Great-niece of Burke, commonly
called the Sublime
She was
Bland, passionate and deeply religious;
Also she painted in water colours,
And sent several pictures to the Exhibition.

She was first cousin to Lady Jones,
And of such is the Kingdom of Heaven.
Anonymous; Pewsey, Bedfordshire

The dead have occasionally seemed to adopt a faintly hectoring tone toward the Almighty:

Here lie I, Martin Elginbrodde.
Ha' mercy o' my soul, Lord Godde,
As I would do were I Lord Godde,
And thou wert Martin Elginbrodde.
Anonymous

while even when a royal prince bit the dust, some observers were unable to work up much spurious loyalty:

Here lies Fred,
Who was alive and is dead:
Had it been his father,
I had much rather;
Had it been his brother,
Still better than another;
Had it been his sister,
No one would have missed her;
Had it been the whole generation,
Still better for the nation:
But since 'tis only Fred,
Who was alive and is dead, —
There's no more to be said.
Anonymous; quoted by Horace Walpole on Frederick, prince of Wales and the House of Hanover 1751

The same sense of ennui has been expressed by others:

Tom Smith is dead, and here he lies,
Nobody laughs and nobody cries;

Where his soul's gone, or how it fares,
Nobody knows, and nobody cares.

Anonymous; Newbury, England 1742

Naturally enough, stronger personalities evoke less indifferent views on their fate in the hereafter. At times the deceased is given the benefit of the doubt —

Here lie the bones of Robert Lowe:
Where he's gone to I don't know.
If the realms of peace and love,
Farewell to happiness above.
If he's gone to a lower level,
I can't congratulate the Devil.

E. Knatchbull-Hugessen on
Robert Lowe

Here Holy Willie's sair-worn clay
Taks up its last abode;
His saul has ta'n some other way —
I fear the left-hand road.

Robert Burns (1759-1796)

ROBERT BURNS

but just as often his fate is not left open to question:

Here lie Willie Michie's banes;
O Satan, when ye tak him,
Gie him the schoolin' o' your weans,
For clever deils he'll mak' em!

Robert Burns (1759-1796) on a
schoolmaster in Cleish Parish,
Kinross-shire

Here lies the body of Bob Dent;
He kicked up his heels and to Hell he went.

Anonymous; Grand Gulf
Cemetery, near Port Gibson,
Miss.

If heav'n be pleas'd when sinners cease to sin,
If hell be pleas'd when souls are damn'd therein,
If earth be pleas'd when it's rid of a knave,
Then all are pleas'd, for Coleman's in his grave.

Anonymous, 1704

In extreme cases, even the demons are not happy to receive one
of their own:

When X deceased and passed below,
Earth jumped for joy. "For you 'tis well,"
Said Nick, "but I should like to know
Why was this monster sent to Hell?"

F. P. Barnard

The foibles of the well-born, the famous and the infamous are
particularly likely to be commemorated in less than complimen-
tary terms. This happy play on words records the passing of a
tactfully unnamed scion of the aristocracy who had committed
a heinous social sin:

256

Here lies
Henry William, twenty-second Lord ———,
In Joyful expectation of the last trump.

> Lord Alvanley (1745-1804) on a
> noble lord who had been
> expelled from society for
> cheating at whist

Those who had held unpopular opinions could provoke violent reactions:

Died in Vermont the profane and
impious Deist Gen. Ethan Allen. . . .
And in Hell he lift up his eyes, being in
Torments.

> Ezra Stiles (1727-1795) on Ethan Allen 1789

But even notorious wrongdoers sometimes prompted a more ambiguous response. The dashing criminal always seems to inspire a sneaking admiration:

Here lies DuVall; reader if male thou art,
Look to thy purse; if female to thy heart.

> Anonymous; Covent Garden
> Church; on highwayman Claude
> DuVall

Although strictly speaking he was not a criminal, an innovative minister of Louis XIV probably fared better than he deserved. Sydney Smith might have approved:

Here lies the father of taxation:
May Heaven, his faults forgiving,
Grant him repose; which he, while living,
Would never grant the nation.

> R. A. Davenport (1777-1852) on Jean Baptiste Colbert

Even the longest and noblest lineage, apparently, is no guarantee against a sticky end:

> *Bright ran thy line, O Galloway,*
> *Thro' many a far-fam'd sire;*
> *So ran the far-fam'd Roman way,*
> *So ended in a mire!*
>> Robert Burns (1759-1796) on Lord Galloway

The spiteful and malicious denizens of the artistic world have naturally enough supplied a wealth of material for lapidary philosophers. A well-known comic actor met an appropriate end:

> *Foote from his earthly stage, alas! is hurl'd;*
> *Death took him off, who took off all the world.*
>> Anonymous; *Dodd's Select*
>> *Epigrams* 1797; on Samuel Foote

Artistic feuds are frequently carried beyond the grave. A brilliant but erratic poet could not let the leading painter of his day rest in peace:

> *O reader behold the philosopher's grave!*
> *He was born quite a fool but he died quite a knave.*
>> William Blake (1757-1827) on Sir Joshua Reynolds

while a critic who had produced a bad-tempered and vindictive epitaph on Samuel Johnson became, in turn, the victim of a nasty little rebuke:

> *Here lies a little ugly nauseous elf,*
> *Who judging only from its wretched self,*
> *Feebly attempted, petulant and vain,*
> *The 'Origin of Evil' to explain.*
>> Anonymous; on Soame Jenyns

Every so often the epitaph is used to poke fun at society. The poet Samuel Butler received meager financial rewards during his lifetime, but a monument was erected to him on his death:

Whilst Butler, needy wretch! was yet alive,
No gen'rous patron would a dinner give:
See him when starved to death, and turn'd to dust,
Presented with a monumental bust!
The poet's fate is here in emblem shown, —
He ask'd for bread, and he receiv'd a stone.
> Samuel Wesley (1810-1876) on
> Samuel Butler

Would-be poets, too, may find that lack of appreciation lingers after them:

Here lies that peerless paper peer Lord Peter,
Who broke the laws of God and man and metre.
> Sir Walter Scott (1771-1832) on
> Patrick ("Peter") Lord Robertson

and the enemies of some authors pen acrimonious but premature epitaphs in undisguised anticipation. G. K. Chesterton had a tendency to pontificate:

Poor G.K.C., his day is past —
Now God will know the truth at last.
> E. V. Lucas (1868-1938) on G. K.
> Chesterton; proposed epitaph

and his critics perceived an unpleasant streak of anti-Semitism in his views:

Here lies Mr. Chesterton,
who to heaven might have gone,
But didn't when he heard the news
That the place was run by Jews.
> Humbert Wolfe (1886-1940) on
> G.K. Chesterton; proposed epitaph

Nor have the discoveries of science always been welcome with open arms. Alexander Pope had celebrated the theories of Newton in a famous couplet:

Nature and Nature's law, lay hid in night:
God said, Let Newton be! *and all was light.*
                                        Alexander Pope (1688-1744)

but a modern observer, contemplating the upheaval in scientific thought, penned a sardonic reply:

It did not last: the Devil, howling Ho!
Let Einstein be! *restored the status quo.*
                                        J. C. Squire (1884-1958) on
                                        Albert Einstein

EINSTEIN

In one fantasy at least, the esoteric mathematician became the victim of his own speculations on the uncertainties of modern life:

Here Einstein lies;
At least, they laid his bier
Just hereabouts —
Or relatively near.

Kensal Green on Albert Einstein

The epitaph has provided countless fond husbands a last chance to express the true depth of marital devotion —

I laid my wife
Beneath this stone,
For her repose
And for my own.

Anonymous; Ottawa graveyard

Here lies my wife,
Here lies she;
Hallelujah!
Hallelujee!

Anonymous; Leeds graveyard; *Norfolk's Epitaphs* 1861

— feelings shared by a great English poet:

Here lies my wife: here let her lie!
Now she's at rest, and so am I.

John Dryden (1631-1700) on his wife

A few short lines can be enough to portray the gripping and sometimes tragic drama of domestic life:

Papa loved mamma
Mamma loved men
Mamma's in the graveyard
Papa's in the pen

Carl Sandburg (1878-1967)

while the burdens of family decision-making are evident even in the graveyard:

Here lies the mother of children seven,
Four on earth and three in heaven;
The three in heaven preferring rather
To die with mother than live with father.

Anonymous; Birmingham graveyard

For some people, the most noteworthy thing in life is their manner of leaving it:

Here lies John Tyrwitt
A learned divine;
He died in a fit
Through drinking port wine
Died 3rd April, 1828, aged 59

Anonymous; Malta 1828

Against his will
Here lies George Hill,
Who from a cliff
Fell down quite stiff.
When it happen'd is not known,
Therefore not mentioned on this stone.

Anonymous; St. Peter's
Churchyard, Isle of Thanet

To the Memory
of
Abraham Beaulieu
Born 15 September
1822
Accidentally shot
4th April 1844
As a mark of affection
from his brother

Anonymous

Nothing in this melancholy chapter of accidents, however, can be quite so affecting as this cautionary tale:

In memory of
THOMAS THATCHER,
A Grenadier of the Ninth Regiment
of Hants Militia, who died of a
violent fever, contracted by drinking
small beer when hot the 12th of May,
1769, aged 26 years. . . .
Here sleeps in peace a Hampshire Grenadier
Who caught his death by drinking cold small beer.
Soldiers, be wise from his untimely fall,
And when ye're hot, drink strong or none at all.

Anonymous; Winchester
Cathedral yard

Given the obvious perils of living, it would seem that this plaintive child did not know when he was well off:

It is so soon that I am done for,
I wonder what I was begun for.

Anonymous; child's grave, Cheltenham

263

The ultimate form of accident insurance appears to have been adopted by a provident Oxfordshire gentleman who clearly believed in taking no chances:

Here lies the body of John Eldred.
At least he will be here when he is dead;
But now at this time he is alive
The 14th August, Sixty Five.
John Eldred; Oxfordshire churchyard 1765

Of all men, politicians are the most open to scorn and ridicule — and it often follows them to the grave. The species as a whole tends to be distinctly unappreciated:

There lies beneath this mossy stone
A politician who
Touched a live issue without gloves,
And never did come to.
Keith Preston

Even obscure politicians find their less attractive qualities under attack. This one was always in too much of a hurry:

Lay aside, all yet dead,
For in the next bed
Reposes the body of Cushing;
He has crowded his way
Through the world, as they say,
And even though dead will keep pushing.
Hanna F. Gould on Caleb Cushing; proposed epitaph

and some invite even stronger disapprobation. Lord Byron loathed Viscount Castlereagh, but with misdirected nineteenth-century delicacy required the reader to supply the missing rhyme:

Posterity will ne'er survey
A nobler grave than this;
Here lies the bones of Castlereagh:
Stop traveller, — ——
Lord Byron (1788-1824)

LORD
BYRON

A long-time member of the British House of Commons summarized the general attitude toward politicians:

Here richly, with ridiculous display,
The Politician's corpse was laid away.
While all of his acquaintance sneered and slanged,
I wept: for I had longed to see him hanged.
Hilaire Belloc (1870-1953)

265

Politics was not the only profession to attract the creators of tombstone literature. The matching of the deceased's occupation to an apt inscription became something of a folk art. Few practitioners were as blatant as this enterprising husband:

Here lies Jane Smith, wife of Thomas Smith, marble cutter. This monument was erected by her husband as a tribute to her memory and a specimen of his work. Monuments of the same style 350 dollars.

Thomas Smith

but the architect of Blenheim Palace was the victim of a suitably heavy-handed figure of speech:

Under this stone, Reader, survey
Dead Sir John Vanbrugh's house of clay.
Lie heavy on him, Earth! for he
Laid many heavy loads on thee!

Abel Evans (1679-1737) on Sir John Vanbrugh

Not many prophecies have been as grotesque as this one about a lady who ran a pottery shop:

Beneath this stone lies Catherine Gray,
Changed to a lifeless lump of clay.
By earth and clay she got her pelf,
And now she's turned to earth herself.
Ye weeping friends let me advise,
Abate your tears and dry your eyes;
For what avails a flood of tears?
Who knows but in a course of years,
In some tall pitcher or brown pan,
She in her shop may be again?

Anonymous; in a Chester, England, church

The ever-waspish Byron could not resist this observation on the fate of a toping carrier:

John Adams lies here, of the parish of Southwell,
A Carrier who carried his can to his mouth well:
He carried so much, and he carried so fast,
He could carry no more — so was carried at last;
For the liquor he drank, being too much for one,
He could not carry off, — so he's now carrion.
                              Lord Byron (1788-1824) on John Adams

and another commentator pointed out the evil effects of social climbing on a weaver who would not stick to his loom:

Geta from wool and weaving first began
Swelling and swelling to a Gentleman;
When he was Gentleman and bravely dight,
He left not swelling till he was a knight:
At last (forgetting what he was at first)
He swole to be a Lord, and then he hurst.
                              Thomas Bastard (1566-1618)

Certain occupations seemed heaven-sent for a satirical dig:

A zealous locksmith died of late,
And did arrive at Heaven's gate.
He stood without, and would not knock,
Because he meant to pick the lock.
                              Anonymous; *Camden's Remains* 1623

including that favorite target, the money-lender:

Here lies old twenty-five percent,
The more he had, the more he lent.

The more he had, the more he craved,
Great God, can this poor soul be saved?
> Anonymous; Nova Scotia 19th century

As popular as a gloss on occupations was a play on names. Generations of epitaph-makers have been unable to resist a pun:

"Fuller's earth."
> Thomas Fuller (1608-1661) on himself

Urn a lively Hood
> Thomas Hood (1835-1874) on himself

Alack, and well-a-day,
Potter himself is turned to clay!
> Anonymous; on Archbishop
> Potter 1747

Here lies a Bond under this tomb
Seal'd and deliver'd to God knows whom.
> Anonymous; *Wit Restored* 1658;
> on Bond the Usurer

Some authors tried a little harder, and produced more ambitious images:

When from the chrysalis of the tomb
I rise in rainbow-colour'd plume,
My weeping friends, ye scarce will know
That I was but a Grubb below.
> Anonymous; *Booth's Epitaphs*
> 1868; on John Grubb

Under this sod
And under these trees
Lieth the body of Solomon Pease.

268

He's not in this hole,
But only his pod;
He shelled out his soul
And went up to God.

Anonymous; Ohio tombstone

What! kill a partridge in the month of May!
Was that done like a sportsman? Eh, Death, eh?

Anonymous; *Norfolk's Epitaphs*
1861; on Mr. Partridge

But there is no question that the energies of some authors have been totally misapplied. Words cannot describe the pedantic wag who is addicted to the Latin pun:

Ars longa, vita brevis.

Anonymous; on Thomas Longbottom

The play on words has always been popular in epitaphs:

These walls, so full of monument and bust,
Show how Bath waters serve to lay the dust.

Henry Harington, M.D.; Abbey
Church, Bath

This line of thought, pursued to its extreme, results in the avowedly comic epitaph. One of these maligns Cobbett's favorite resort:

Here lie I and my four daughters,
Killed by drinking Cheltenham waters.
Had we but stuck to Epsom salts,
We wouldn't have been in these here vaults.

Anonymous; *Norfolk's Epitaphs* 1861

269

while another attests to the strength and endurance of family affection:

Beneath this stone, in hopes of Zion,
Doth lie the landlord of the Lion;
His son keeps on the business still,
Resigned unto the heavenly will.

>   Anonymous; *Fairley's*
>   *Epitaphiana* 1875; on an
>   innkeeper

and yet another comments on persistence in the face of apparently overwhelming odds:

Here lies all that remains of Charlotte,
Born a virgin, died a harlot.
For sixteen years she kept her virginity,
A marvellous thing for this vicinity.

>   Anonymous; Welland, Ont.

Today's liberated women would no doubt deplore the conditions described by this oppressed sister — but one wonders if they are entirely obsolete:

Here lies a poor woman who always was tired;
She lived in a house where help was not hired.
Her last words on earth were: "Dear friends, I am going
Where washing ain't done, nor sweeping, nor sewing:
But everything there is exact to my wishes;
For where they don't eat there's no washing of dishes. . . .
Don't mourn for me now; don't mourn for me never —
I'm going to do nothing for ever and ever."

>   Anonymous; *The Tired Woman's Epitaph*

One way of striking back at the epitaph-maker is to write one's own. Tradition has it that the Bard himself composed his memorial, although the quality of the verse speaks against it:

Good friend for Jesus sake, forebaere,
To dig the dust encloased heare
Blest be ye man yt spares thes stones,
And curst be he yt moves my bones.
Shakespeare's epitaph; Stratford-on-Avon

Many intrepid souls have commended their own best qualities to posterity:

When I am dead, I hope it may be said:
"His sins were scarlet but his books were read."
Hilaire Belloc (1870-1953)

He reads but he cannot speak Spanish,
He cannot abide ginger beer:
Ere the days of his pilgrimage vanish,
How pleasant to know Mr. Lear!
Edward Lear (1812-1888)

A faintly self-deprecatory air is considered de rigueur:

Here lies one who meant well, tried a little, failed much.
Robert Louis Stevenson (1850-1894)

although few have had such good reason for self-criticism as the emperor Joseph:

Let my epitaph be, "Here lies Joseph, who failed in everything
he undertook."
Joseph II, Holy Roman Emperor 1790

271

The contemplation of a better world did not seem to alarm H. L. Mencken:

If, after I depart this vale, you remember me and have some thought to please my ghost, forgive some sinner and wink your eye at a homely girl.

H. L. Mencken (1880-1956)

But perhaps the most profound comment on the hereafter was expressed by a notable curmudgeon:

On the whole, I'd rather be in Philadelphia.

W. C. Fields (1880-1946)

While the frivolous epitaph has its place, the glory of the art undoubtedly lies in the full-blown, carefully constructed, total condemnation of one's fellow man. Few examples can match this balanced and reasoned eighteenth-century excoriation of a thorough-going villain:

HERE *continueth to rot*
The Body of FRANCIS CHARTRES,
Who with inflexible constancy,
and Inimitable Uniformity of Life
Persisted
In spite of Age and Infirmities
In the practice of Every Human Vice;
Excepting Prodigality and Hypocrisy:
His insatiable Avarice exempted him from the first,
His matchless Impudence from the second.
Nor was he more singular
in the undeviating Pravity of his Manners
Than successful
In Accumulating WEALTH . . .

He was the only Person of his Time
Who cou'd cheat without the Mask of Honesty
Retain his Primeval Meanness
When possess'd of Ten Thousand a Year
And having daily deserved the Gibbet for what he did,
Was at last condemn'd to it for what he could not do.

Dr. John Arbuthnot (1667-1735)
on Francis Chartres, gambler,
brothel-keeper, money-lender

Only the most impenitent of sinners would not feel the sting of such a posthumous indictment. But occasionally a counteroffensive is launched from beyond the grave. The final will and testament has provided a golden opportunity for some hardy individualists to have, truly, the last word.

A goodly number of those who were about to die apparently set about it in a distinctly uncharitable mood, nursing to the end their grievances against their nearest and dearest. One Samuel Baldwin was buried at sea in 1736; in choosing this mode of interment he managed to score off his wife one final time, Mrs. Baldwin having promised to dance on his grave if she survived him. The settling of marital accounts shows a record of continually diminishing returns:

I give to Elizabeth Parker the sum of £50, whom, through my foolish fondness, I made my wife; and who in return has not spared, most unjustly, to accuse me of every crime regarding human nature, save highway-robbery.

Charles Parker, 1785

I do give and bequeath to Mary Davis the sum of five shillings, which is sufficient to enable her to get drunk for the last time at my expense.

David Davis, 1788

I give unto my wife Mary Darley, for picking my pocket of 60 guineas, and taking up money in my name, the sum of one shilling.

William Darley, 1794

The serpent's tooth of filial ingratitude has stung many a father. Some have struck back:

To my only son, who never would follow my advice, and has treated me rudely in many circumstances, I give him nothing.

Richard Crashaw, 1810

But one noble and inventive parent left his wayward boy a particularly grisly memorial:

I leave my right hand, to be cut off after my death, to my son Lord Audley; in hopes that such a sight may remind him of his duty to God, after having so long abandoned the duty he owed to a father who once affectionately loved him.

Philip Thicknesse, 1793

The effect of this kind remembrance on young Audley has not been recorded.

The eccentric William "Tiger" Dunlop was a prominent figure in the settlement of Ontario, and gathered around him a large family. The temptation to take posthumous potshots at his loved ones proved too much for him, as witness his famous last will and testament:

In the name of God. Amen.

I, William Dunlop, of Gairbraid, in the Township of Colborne, County and District of Huron, Western Canada, Esquire, being in sound health of body, and my mind just as usual (which my friends who flatter me say is no great shakes at the best of times), do make this my last Will and Testament as follows, revoking, of course, all former Wills:

I leave the property of Gairbraid, and all other landed property I may die possessed of, to my sisters Helen Boyle Story and Elizabeth Boyle Dunlop; the former because she is married to a minister whom (God help him) she henpecks. The latter because she is married to nobody, nor is she like to be, for she is an old maid, and not market-rife. . . .

I leave my silver tankard to the eldest son of old John, as the representative of the family. I would have left it to old John himself, but he would melt it down to make temperance medals, and that would be sacrilege — however, I leave my big horn snuffbox to him; he can only make temperance horn spoons out of that. . . .

I also leave my late brother's watch to my brother Sandy, exhorting him at the same time to give up Whiggery, Radicalism, and all other sins that do most easily beset him. . . .

I leave Parson Chevasse (Magg's husband), the snuff-box I got from the Sarnia Militia, as a small token of my gratitude for the service he has done the family in taking a sister that no man of taste would have taken.

I leave John Caddle a silver teapot, to the end that he may drink tea therefrom to comfort him under the affliction of a slatternly wife.

I leave my books to my brother Andrew, because he has been so long a Jungley Wallah, that he may learn to read with them. . . .

In witness whereof I have hereunto set my hand and seal the thirty-first day of August, in the year of our Lord one thousand eight hundred and forty-two.

W. DUNLOP

William Dunlop (1792-1848)

275

Tiger Dunlop must have died a happy man. What better ending for a true curmudgeon than to have the last word — an unkind one?

Here lies Aretino, Tuscan poet
Who spoke evil of everyone but God,
Giving the excuse, "I never knew Him."
                                        Anonymous

Index of Authors and Sources

281

Index of Subjects

Chamberlain, Joseph: 132-3
Chamberlain, Neville: 139
Charles I: 59
Charles II: 59, 119
Charles, Francis: 273
Chatham, William Pitt (the elder),
Lord: 167
Chatterton, Thomas: 181
Chaucer, Geoffrey: 24
Cheltenham: 221
Chesterfield, Lord: 52-3
Chesterton, G.K.: 183, 259
Chicago: 106
Chinese, the: 114
Church, the: 54, 55
Churchill, Randolph: 170
Churchill, Winston: 140-42
Clark, Joe: 156
Clarke, Creston: 85
Clay, Henry: 124-25
Cleveland, Grover: 129, 188
Cobbert, William: 218, 224
Colbert, Jean Baptiste: 257
Coleridge, Samuel Taylor: 63, 67, 234
Collins, Churton: 21, 67
Confederation, Canadian: 150-1
Congressmen, U.S.: 34, 77, 122, 128
Conkling, Rosco: 172
Conrad, Joseph: 185
Conservatives, British: 141
Coolidge, Calvin: 131, 172
Cootle, Amos: 63
Country living: 55
Cranmer, Archbistop Thomas: 222
Cripps, Sir Stafford: 140, 171
Critics: 21, 61, 66-67
Cromwell, Oliver: 121
Cushing, Caleb: 261
Curses: 24-26, 121

Dante Alighieri: 180
Darley, Mary: 273

Darwin, Charles: 68
Davies, Scrope: 201
Davis, Jefferson: 128
Davis, Mary: 273
Davy, Humphrey: 177
De Gaulle, Charles: 175
De Mille, Cecil b. 31
Democracy: 122, 124-25, 132,
144, 160
Democrats, U.S.: 159-60
Demosthenes: 166
Dent, Bob: 256
Depew, Chauncey: 169, 170
De Valera, Eamon: 22
Dewey, Thomas E.: 133, 173
Dickens, Charles: 76, 245
Difenbaker, John C.: 156
Disraeli, Benjamin: 138
Donne, John: 164
Douglas, Stephen A.: 127, 189
Dramatic criticism: 21, 22, 45, 47,
85-86
Dundas, Earl of: 134
Drey, O.R.: 200
Dryden, Elizabeth: 261
Duoro, Lord: 229
Durham, Lord: 148
Duvall, Clauce: 257

Earp, Thomas W.: 85
East India Company: 135, 212
Eden, Anthony: 142, 143
Edward VII: 189
Einstein, Albert: 41, 260, 261
Eldred, John: 261
Elginbrodde, Martin: 254
Eliot, Thomas Stearns: 185
Ely, Bishop of: 121
Emerson, Ralph Waldo: 20, 70-1
Enemues: 21, 32, 75
England and the English: 21, 47, 57,
75, 85, 90-96, 97-8, 103, 104,

285

The Author wishes to thank the following for permission to reprint material included in this book: Sir Rupert Hart-Davis for extracts by Max Beerbohm. Harper & Row Publishers, Inc. for extracts by Robert Benchley. The Estate of the late E.C. Bentley and A.P. Watt Ltd. For extracts from two poems "Geoffrey Chaucer" and "George the Third" by E.C. Bentley. George Allen & Unwin Ltd. and Barnes & Noble for extracts from Letters From England by Karel Capek. William Heinemann Ltd. for extracts from The Life and Letters of sir Edmond Gosse by Evan Charteris. Dodd Mead & Co. and A.P. Watt Ltd. for two lines of poetry by G.K. Chesterton. John Robert Colombo for extracts from Colombo s Concise Canadian Quotations Edmonton Hurtig Publishers 1976, and "Oh Canada" from The Sad Truths, Toronia: Peter Marvin Associates, 1974. Syndication International Ltd. for extracts from Boiled Cabbage by William Connor. P.M.A. Books for extracts from I Never Say Anything Provocative, edited by Margaret Wente (1975). Simon & Schuster, a Division of Gulf & Western Corporation, for extracts from With Malice Towards Some by Margaret Halsey (Copyright C 1938, 1965 by Margaret Halsey). The Sterling Lord Agency, Inc. for extracts from The Fine Art of Political Wit by Leon A. Harris. The Society of Authors as literary representatives of the Estate of A.E. Houseman for extracts from A.E. Houseman s work. The Washington Post for extracts by Paul Hume. Mrs. Dorinda Maxse for extracts by Henry Arthur Jones. Clarke, Irwin & Company Ltd. for extracts from The Firebrand by William Kilbourn. The National Trust and A.P. Watt Ltd. for extracts from two poems by Rudyard Kipling. Doubleday & Company, Inc. for extract from The Cutting Edge by Louis Kronenberger (Copyright C 1970 by Louis Kronenberger). Faber & Faber Ltd. for extracts from The Whitsun Weddings by Philip Larkin. The Macmillan Company of Canada Ltd. and Houghton Mifflin Company for the poem "William Lyon Mackenzie King" from Alligator Pie by Dennis Lee (Copyright C 1974 by Dennis Lee). The Author and the author s agents, Scott Meredith Library Agency, Inc. 845 Third Avenue, New York, New York 1002 for extracts from Some Notes on the 1960 Democratic Convention by Norman Mailer. The John Hopkins University Press for extracts from H.C. Menchen, A Carnival of Buncombe by Malcolm Moos. Curtis Brown, Inc. and Little Brown and Co. for the poem "Further Reflections on Parsley" by Ogden Nash (Copyright C 1942, 1958 by Ogden Nash). Berbert V. Prochnow for extracts from A Treasury of Humorous Quotations by Herbert V. Prochnow and Herbert V. Prochnow Jr. George Allen & Unwin Ltd. for extracts from Sceptical Essays by Bertrand Russell. Frank R. Scott for an extract from Selected Poems. The society of Authors on behalf of the Bernard Shaw Estate for extracts from Bernard Shaw s work. Mrs. Iris Wise, Macmillan, London and Basingstoke. The Macmillan Company of Canada Ltd. and Macmillan Publishing Co., Inc. for an excerpt from Collected Poems of James Stephens. The Society of Authors as agents for The Strachey Trust for extracts by Lytton Scrachey. The New Yorker Magazine, Inc. for a caption by F.B. White to a cartoon by Carl Rose, Copyright C 1956 by The New Yorker Magazine, Inc.

291